I Am Anointed For This

AWAKE TO YOUR DESTINY

VOLUME 2

Apostle Dr. Nadine Manning

I Am Anointed For This

Awake To Your Destiny

Volume 2

Copyright © December 06, 2014

By Apostle Dr. Nadine Manning

ISBN 978-0989836913

Printed in the USA by Prophetic in Warfare Deliverance & Worship Tabernacle in association with Kingdom Graphics Designo Inc.

P.O. Box 343, Millville, New Jersey 08332

propheticinwarfare@gmail.com

Contents

Gratefulness

I would like to dedicate this book to the world best mother, Dorothy Nicholas, for, bringing me into to the world. You are anointed for this. You are truly a woman of strength, endurance, and tenacity. We have been through a few stormy wind experiences together during my eleven years living in the United States. A woman of excellence, and the Lord inaugurate you a *"Pioneer Woman"*.

A pioneer woman is a woman with fireproof faith. Regardless, of what life throws at her, she bounces right back, she is **"Anointed For This.**" She sees the light always at the end of the tunnel. I gather now, where I get my virtue from, separate and apart from Jesus being my rock you have taught me how to be a virtuous woman. Thank you for encouraging me to do what God has called me to do for the Kingdom and for His Glory. Thank you for being there for the children and myself. Most of all, you accepted Pastor Dr. Richard Manning as your son-in-law, and loved and cared for him as your own son. Your relationship was one to be admired. Thank you for being there for me, as a confidant, when I need someone to share ministry moments with.

I also dedicate this book to my dad, who is also a support and a great help during Richard's challenge with his health. Thank you for your patience, love and service you gave not just to your children, but to the other children you raised and sent to school and college that were not your own. Heaven has both your reward in Jesus name.

Last but not the least, in loving memory of the late, Pastor Dr. Richard Manning, February 15, 1969 to May 31st, 2014. Without the experiences gained during our union this book would not have been possible. Your legacy lives on in your children. The life you lived while on earth was one of a firm persuasion according to Romans 8:38-39 and has inspired and given me the tenacity to move forward as well as run with the vision.

"38 For I am persuaded, that neither death, nor life, nor angels, nor principalities, nor powers, nor things present, nor things to come, 39 Nor height, nor depth, nor any other creature, shall be able to separate us from the love of God, which is in Christ Jesus our Lord."

Foreword

I just want to say, to God be the glory, honor and praise, for this precious seed that He has given unto me. Not because I am her mother why I am saying these words about her, but because I have seen that God's hand is upon her from a very tender age as a child. God had called her from the very first time she said yes to Him. He placed His mantle upon her to be a Prophet and an Apostle to the nation.

Apostle Dr. Nadine Manning is a devoted woman of God's word [The Bible]. She goes very deep into God's word to know how to impart it to the people, she is a no nonsense woman when it comes to God's business. She puts the things of God first. I can tell you that Dr. Apostle Nadine Manning is a no nonsense, without compromise carrier of the inspired word of God as Isaiah 61 declares,

>*"The Spirit of the Lord God is upon me; because the Lord hath anointed me to preach good tidings unto the meek; he hath sent me to bind up the brokenhearted, to proclaim liberty to*

the captives, and the opening of the prison to them that are bound; 2 To proclaim the acceptable year of the Lord, and the day of vengeance of our God; to comfort all that mourn; 3 To appoint unto them that mourn in Zion, to give unto them beauty for ashes, the oil of joy for mourning, the garment of praise for the spirit of heaviness; that they might be called trees of righteousness, the planting of the Lord, that he might be glorified."

So also, this mantle of the good news of Salvation is given to Apostle Dr. Nadine Manning. Apostle is a friend and an encourager, always giving others an inspiring word from the Lord. If you come in contact with her, you will never be the same. She pushes you beyond what I can describe as being an average Christian, to desiring more of God and to be an extraordinary servant.

Her demonstration of the power of God through the preached word edifies you and pushes you to the limit so you can reach your destiny, and discover the supernatural power of God through His word. Her passion for worship, prayer and intercession is evident in her life, and ministry globally as well as in our local church, Prophetic in Warfare Deliverance and Worship Tabernacle, where she and her late husband, Pastor Dr. Richard Manning are founders.

This same tenacity and passion flows and is poured out not only through the proclamations or preached word from Apostle Dr. Nadine [My daughter], but also in her writings. So if you have read Volume 1 of **"Awake to Your Destiny"**, entitled ***"The Mind of Christ"***, I guess you can't wait to read Volume 2, ***"I Am Anointed for This."*** I pray that this book will push you further and deeper in the revelation of the most high God.

Jeremiah 1:4-6 says that, God called Jeremiah even before he was formed in his mother's womb and sanctified him to be a prophet to the nations. Like Jeremiah, God has called Dr. Apostle Nadine Manning and she did not reject the call. She said *"Yes Lord, hear am I send me"*. So DON'T DELAY! Let Volume 2 of Awake to Your Destiny, be a must get also for your library.

Missionary Dorothy Nicholas [Mom]

Setting the Atmosphere

The objective of this book is to provoke change. It is to encourage you to 'WALK IT OUT.' Walk it out means make headway, to pursue a course of action. When God visited Jeremiah and spoke to him, mentally, he did not feel prepared or ready for the purpose. He didn't think it was the right time either, based on what he said in verse 6, **W"O Sovereign Lord," I said, "I can't speak for you! I'm too young!"** But God was simply trying to tell him in verse 5 that, **"You Are Anointed For This!"**

> **"I knew you before I formed you in your mother's womb. Before you were born I set you apart and appointed you as my prophet to the nations."**

All God requires you to do is pay attention to the details. One thing is consistent in a winner, is that they pay attention to details. Jeremiah 1:7 reveals further that God reassured Him, by giving him details,

> **"Say not, that I am a child for thou shalt go to all that I shall send thee, and whatsoever I command thee thou shalt**

speak. 8 Be not afraid of their faces for I shall be with thee to deliver thee."

As you read this book, it will reassure you to pick back up where you left of with your purpose, the gifts, talents or specific assignment the Lord has given you. It may have been a direct assignment from the Lord, or one delegated to you by your leader, be it your Pastor, or a secular leader. But understand that there is supernatural abundance from the Lord that is being released in this season and you need to position yourself to discern the time and the season you are in and know that God already predestinated the weight of the glory you will carry.

See, I have this day set thee over the nations and over the kingdoms, to root out, and to pull down, and to destroy, and to throw down, to build, and to plant" [Jeremiah 1:10].

Don't let the inner struggles or outward stormy trials and turbulence deter you from pressing into the glory and walk out your purpose and your assignment for the Lord. Whatever you are called to be: - An usher, an "A" student, Psalmist, songwriter, a preacher, a great wife or husband or a preacher, you have been uniquely anointed for this.

Don't run from the blessings, favor, or assignment God is releasing to you, embrace the next dimension with confidence knowing that:
"I AM ANOINTED FOR THIS."
Stay faithful, even under pressure because what didn't kill you is getting ready to elevate you. It did not destroy you therefore it is shifting you into your next dimension. Like David, God is changing the guards, and His Spirit is hovering across the globe in search for the next king. You are next. An Apostolic anointing of that of Samuel is unleashed to discover you in this season. This is your season of discovery. Decree it right now: - *"This is my season of discovery and* ***"I Am Anointed For This"***.

> ***"In the same way all seven of Jesse's sons were presented to Samuel. But Samuel said to Jesse, "The Lord has not chosen any of these." 11 Then Samuel asked, "Are these all the sons you have?" "There is still the youngest," Jesse replied. "But he's out in the fields watching the sheep and goats." "Send for him at once," Samuel said. "We will not sit down to eat until he arrives." 12 So Jesse sent for him. He was dark and handsome, with beautiful eyes. And the Lord said, "<u>This is the one; anoint him.</u>"*** [1 Samuel 10:10-12]

INTRODUCTION

I Am Anointed For This

<u>Jeremiah 1:5–10</u>

"Before I formed thee in the belly I knew thee; and before thou camest forth out of the womb I sanctified thee, and I ordained thee a prophet unto the nations. 6 Then said I, Ah, Lord God! behold, I cannot speak: for I am a child. 7 But the Lord said unto me, Say not, I am a child: for thou shalt go to all that I shall send thee, and whatsoever I command thee thou shalt speak. 8 Be not afraid of their faces: for I am with thee to deliver thee, saith the Lord. 9 Then the Lord put forth his hand, and touched my mouth. And the Lord said unto me, Behold, I have put my words in thy mouth. 10 See, I have this day set thee over the nations and over the kingdoms, to root out, and to

pull down, and to destroy, and to throw down, to build, and to plant".

- **<u>Anoint means</u>**: - To pour oil or ointment onto a person or object.
- The word first appears in **<u>Genesis 31:13</u>** **"I am the God who appeared to you at Bethel,* the place where you anointed the pillar of stone and made your vow to me. Now get ready and leave this country and return to the land of your birth."**
- Jacob is seen pouring oil on the stone of Bethel (Genesis 28:18-19). At a later time the ceremony was repeated (Genesis 35:9-15).
- The religious ceremony meant entrance into sacred use.
- As a religious act, the anointing was meant to provide the anointed one with the quality of the deity.
- Deity speaks to a Divine Being. We serve the supreme God of the Universe, who sent His son to die in our place, so we can have life and life more abundantly.
- As described above, when you are anointed, 'it is meant to provide the quality of the deity [divine God, our Savior].

- The anointing takes on the quality of the deity (which is Christ Himself.) This means: - the class, superiority, excellence, value, feature our worth of the God we serve.
- When you are *"Anointed For This"* you take on the quality, class, and authority of Jesus Christ himself.

St. John 1:1-4, 9 &12, ***"In the beginning was the Word, and the Word was with God, and the Word was God. 2 The same was in the beginning with God. 3 All things were made by him; and without him was not anything made that was made. 4 In him was life; and the life was the light of men. 9 "That was the true Light, which lighteth every man that cometh into the world. 12 "But as many as received him, to them gave he power to become the sons of God, even to them that believe on his name:"***

When we receive Jesus Christ as our Lord and Savior we receive the indwelling Holy Spirit, our comforter. He is the *"Anointed One"*. Jesus Christ has fulfilled the three ojffices of prophet, priest, and king throughout the scriptures. *"He is, supremely, God's Anointed One."* He is the "Messiah". This is the term for "anointed one" derived directly from the Hebrew word for anointed; "Christ" is the same title derived from the Greek word for "anointee." Jesus Christ, the Holy Spirit is our anointee, and we are filled with His worth, value, excellence, and features. That's right, declare it, ***"I Am Anointed For This"*** filled with is purpose, assignment and divine destiny.

St. John 1:12 tells us that ***"For as many have received Him to them gave he power to become the sons of God"***. The Messiah, supremely, God's Anointed one comes to live on the inside of us when we believe on His name and accept Him as our Lord and Savior. Then the process of sanctification begins. As you desire the sincere milk of the word to grow their by, God begins to prepare you and build your faith through a series of test and trial to be His witness to the world.

> *"My brethren, count it all joy when ye fall into divers temptations; 3 knowing this, that the trying of your faith worketh patience. 4 But let patience have her perfect work, that ye may be perfect and entire, wanting nothing."*
> [James 1:2-4].

You begin to grow and mature as you begin to yield yourself increasingly to the Lord. To each is given a measure of grace to function in the body of Christ.

Ephesians 4:7

> *"But unto every one of us is given grace according to the measure of the gift of Christ"* [KJV].

> *But that doesn't mean you should all look and speak and act the same. Out of the generosity of Christ, each of us is given his own gift"* [The Message].

The level and degree to which God will use you is already pre-determined by God.

The things you will endure, God already made a way of escape. But understand that all the things you have gone through or will go through will prepare you for the anointing that you will carry. When you endure the test and trial to walk it out with the Lord your light will glow or shine in the darkness and people will see their sense of purpose and direction through your life.

You may be asking the question, how do they get their sense of direction through my trials and test? They observe your spiritual life and discern how you "Walk It Out" by faith and handle situations when they come your way. So how you handle your test, trials and difficult circumstances even your past affects those around you for good or bad. I lost my late husband: - Pastor Dr. Richard Manning on May 31st 2014, to date it is approximately six (6) months. Just today, December 12, 2014, I received a card and a one hundred ($100) seed sent by another Pastor going through her **"I Am Anointed For This"** Test". Her message sent to me with the card was, *"I have been following you from Facebook, and you have blessed me, you are a strong woman of God!"*

Someone is admiring your courage and tenacity during your test! How you handle the test, proves ***"I Am Anointed For This"***

I had to follow the leading of God's voice even in the midst of turmoil, despair and yes devastation and loss of my best friend. Someone, I thought I would grow old with. His life was cut short at forty-five (45) years old and I am left a widow with four (4) children.

I've received many words of encouragement, how strong I am, and prophecies that I will marry again. I receive and believe the word of the Lord, but I still need God's grace to "LOVE" again. It's like starting all over again, as the Lord describe it as ***"My New Season!"*** It is like learning to walk and talk all over again. This test in the loss of my late-husband is a proven ground for embracing the next dimension to see if I am really ***"Anointed For This."***

Ruth had to walk it out, when she lost her husband. She had to journey by faith into a land where she was a stranger. How uncomfortable is that. She was a young widow, who must be proven in this season if she is really, ***"Anointed For This."***

Because she was willing to *"Walk It Out"* by faith with God, she walked into greater wealth as she positioned to glean in the field of Boaz. Your trial or test has positioned you for a "SUPERNSTURAL TURNAROUND." As she gleaned in the field of Boaz, where several women work every day, Boaz took notice of her, and gave her special favors in the field and watched over her.

The end result was, Ruth married Boaz, a wealthy man, a King's Man Redeemer and the lineage through whom the Son of God, Jesus Christ came to bring healing, deliverance and salvation to us.

Someone is watching how you handle your loss, it may not be the death of a loved one as in my case, but whatever shape or form your test comes in, it is your proven ground for you to declare in the end, ***"I Am Anointed For This."*** Remember this, your past mistakes, loss, trials or storm can turn into triumph and victories if you trust God in these situations and use them to overcome future obstacles possible similar or greater.

Be reminded also, in the Book of Daniel that the life of Daniel exemplifies one of bravery. He was bold and obedient to his commitment as well as dedication to serve the Lord. Regardless of the pits, the obstacles and traps, he maintained his stance in the Lord. God not only delivered Daniel, but used him as an oracle of the faith and set before him open doors that no man could shut.

Declare it today, **"I am Anointed For This."** The anointing God designed for your life comes out of the process or series of tests, trials and battles you have to endure! But remember this one thing, our Lord and Savior, Jesus Christ has already overcame these things for us through His shed blood on the cross. Make that declaration of faith right now!

"I am not fighting for victory, I am fighting in victory, and" "I Am Anointed For This."

1 John 5:14 **"And this is the confidence that we have in him that, if we ask any thing according to his will, he heareth us:"**

Revelations 12:11 **"They won the victory over him because of the blood of the lamb and the word of their testimony.**

They didn't love their life so much that they refused to give it up."

1 John 5:5 *"Who wins the victory over the world? Isn't it the person who believes that Jesus is the Son of God?"*

CHAPTER 1

Obey God

When God gives you an assignment, He has already predetermined the anointing for the task. Just as He spoke to Jeremiah, that his anointing was predetermined before his formation in his mother's womb. Likewise, the Lord has predetermined your destiny, kingdom purpose and assignment. In fact, long before you discover what your specific call or placement is in the Kingdom, God has already set the path our course your life would take.

"For I know the plans I have for you," says the Lord. They are plans for good and not for disaster, to give you a future and a hope" [Jeremiah 29:11].

All you need to do is obey God. The life experiences, tests, trials, storms and disappointments are all a part of what make you the candidate for the anointing to function and carry out that assignment. It helps to push or birth out your ultimate purpose and destiny.

We will look at Noah, whose world was taken over by evil, violence and corruption – in many ways, not unlike our world today. It was so bad that God was sorrowful for what humankind had chosen for themselves, just as parents feel sorrow when their children chooses to do wrong. Noah and his family were the only ones who remained willing to follow after God and do His will.

Are you willing to follow after God and do His will regardless of what the majority is doing or saying contrary to the truth of God's word? Some may be reading this book that can identify with being the only one saved in your family or the first to be saved in your family. It poses such a spiritual challenge, but this chapter is here to remind you to obey God, and declare, **"I AM ANOINTED FOR THIS"**.

God chose Noah and his family to be a remnant of His creation, to be immune to the harsh judgment He had prepared for those who refused to obey Him and lead Godly lives. He was mocked, jeered and ridiculed because of the task or assignment given to him, yet he kept his focus on the specific instructions given to him with confidence that, ***"I Am Anointed For This."***

Noah was a farmer, a shipbuilder, a zookeeper and the only evangelist. The task given to him by God was to build a gigantic ark and to warn the people of the upcoming flood. Building the ark and warning the people was a great undertaking that required a great deal of faith and obedience.

> Hebrews 11:7 [NLV] ***"Because Noah had faith, he built a large boat for his family. God told him what was going to happen. His faith made him hear God speak and he obeyed. His family was saved from death because he built the boat. In this way, Noah showed the world how sinful it was. Noah became right with God because of his faith in God."***

Noah's eyes were not fixed on the worldly, evil desires of those around him. Instead, his focus and dedication was on growing in his relationship with God.

When you are ***"Anointed For This"*** your focus will never be on your struggles or challenges. Even though, it is evident that they exist. Your focus is always to please and obey the Father as well as to carry out His wishes. What God instructed Noah to do was Noah's highest priority.

You can identify your weakness and challenges all you want like Jeremiah, but when you are anointed to do a specific assignment you will feel a persuasive love and a driving force of the Holy Spirit power impelling you to do what thus saith the Lord. What God instruct you to do should be your highest priority. God honors obedience. Honor means elevation or promotion. Elevation comes only through serving out of love and obedience to God. The Message version says,

> ***"By faith, Noah built a ship in the middle of dry land. He was warned about something he couldn't see, and acted on what he was told. The result? His family was saved. His act of faith drew a sharp line between the evil of the unbelieving world and the***

> ***rightness of the believing world.
> As a result, Noah became intimate
> with God.***"

Noah enjoyed the relationship he had with God. The exchange he had with God as he spent time with him, allowed him to be focused. Noah confided in God, and received instruction from Him. While others saw Noah as plain crazy, God honored his behavior.

Make No Excuses

Genesis 7:5 [KJV] says, ***"And Noah did according to all that the Lord commanded him."***
Obeying God means **"MAKE NO EXCUSES"**. That is the one thing that sets Noah apart from the rest of humankind. It was his "NO EXCUSE" attitude. It was very possible God approached other men and women besides Noah to build the ark. Perhaps they offered excuses why they couldn't serve Him. Has your Pastor, Bishop, Apostle or your Boss ask you to carry out certain task that you think was beyond your scope or ability to accomplish?

Perhaps, God did ask others but they offered excuses about why they couldn't serve Him or carry out the assignment. What is God requiring you to do for Him? You are anointed for the task, or the Lord would not have designated you for the assignment.

Noah did everything God ask of Him without complaints or questions and very likely he got very busy doing the assignment of building the ark right away or without delay. We may think we can excuse ourselves from God's service because we think it's more convenient for someone else to tackle it. Maybe your attitude is, *'there is someone else better educated or better qualified to do the job.'* Or maybe, you don't think it fits your title and persona.

Or maybe you are just boldly resisting submission to God' or his delegated authority which could be your Pastor, boss, parent, guardian or spouse. But God doesn't ask us to come prepared. He just asks us to come eagerly to do the work according to His standards. It was God, not Noah that closed the door to the ark. Just as God set up a covenant with Noah, His designated purpose and destiny for your life requires an agreement. I hear the Lord saying, I need another **'YES'**.

Right now, I hear the Lord saying the ground you are standing on seems or appears familiar because of the people that are around you. But the truth is, everything around you has changed. There is a shift taking place in your life. God is shifting out some people from your sphere of influence and shifting you into a new place not just naturally but spiritually.

Don't abort your purpose, "DESTINY IS CALLING YOU", and the ground beneath you feels familiar! But initiated through the supernatural realm, everything has changed, based on the instructions God has given you for your life, purpose and divine assignment. It was Noah's obedience to specific details and direction that not only saved his life, but also his family.

Three (3) years ago, I moved in obedience to the instructions God gave me, to launch a ministry in this region called, "Prophetic in Warfare Deliverance and Worship Tabernacle." Many laughed, scoffed and ridiculed us. Moreover, it seems like a network was set up against us to make us feel abandoned and alone. But Ephesians chapter 6:12 remain our cover.

Our wrestle is not against man [flesh and blood], but against principalities and powers. If you want to successfully defeat the enemy, just walk in obedience. Your obedience is a branding on your life, indicating that, ***"I Am Anointed For This." "THIS"*** means, the assignment, the blessings or promises and ultimate destiny God has in store for you.

We are in our third (3rd.) year of ministry and have touched so many lives globally by walking in obedience. Now we cover 5 churches in the Philippines and an Outreach Ministry in Jamaica, as well as ministry in Canada that we provide Apostolic Counsel to. If I had listened to the majority, many lives that were at stake would not have received their breakthrough or deliverance. Did I get discouraged, yes, several times, but like Jeremiah, ***"I Am Anointed For This"*** and I feel like the fire of the Lord is shut up in my bones enthralling me to keep moving forward.

> ***"Then I said, "I will not make mention of Him, Nor speak anymore in His name." But His word was in my heart like a burning fire; Shut up in my***

bones; I was weary of holding it back, And I could not [Jeremiah 20:9, NKJV].

"You pushed me into this, God, and I let you do it. You were too much for me. And now I'm a public joke. They all poke fun at me. Every time I open my mouth I'm shouting, "Murder!" or "Rape!" And all I get for my God-warnings are insults and contempt. But if I say, "Forget it! No more God-Messages from me!" The words are fire in my belly, a burning in my bones" [Jeremiah 20:9, The Message]

Your obedience to the instructions God has given you for your life, purpose and divine assignment positions you to bring deliverance to others. Someone is carefully observing your movements and is also destined to move with you into their new season. There is a remnant [minority] that will be connected to you that will catapult with you into your new season. There are others watching from a far off, that will also enter supernaturally, because of your obedience and testimony they observe coming from your life. How is that Apostle Dr. Nadine?

Because they too have like-mind to follow the Lord and do His blessed will.

Don't worry about those who don't understand your actions or movements. You may look like you are in the minority, but **"Stand Strong in the Minority"** with confidence that ***"I Am Anointed For This."*** It is often tempting to relinquish your position on the assignment or disobey God's instruction or direction for your life when it appears that you are in the minority. The instruction may not necessarily be for ministry, but whom you should to marry. Maybe it is an anointed woman or man but they have a child or children and you insist you want a meek, quiet damsel or a wealthy man who lack the wisdom, maturity and anointing to make you compatible in ministry.

Will you marry out of God's will to fit the crowd or do you rather stay in the minority and find favor in God's eyes. You are anointed for this, so "Stand Strong in the Minority" like Noah's admirably example. God expects us to stand for what is right. What is right is **"WHATEVER JESUS TELLS YOU TO DO ~ DO IT!"**

Like Noah stick to your guns and finish your assignment. Walk it out by faith and watch the vision come to fruition. Moreover, when you walk in obedience you will find favor in the eyes of the Lord.

> ***The Lord said, I will blot out man whom I have created from the face of the land, from man to animals to creeping things and to birds of the sky; for I am sorry that I have made them. But Noah found favor in the eyes of the Lord"*** [Genesis 6:7-8].

Be A God-Pleaser for 2015 and Beyond

Are you more concerned about man's acceptance or approval or are you yielded to the will of God for your life with a complete **"YES."** When God speaks and directs our path it is a **"Walk of Faith!"** Let him choose your friends, your husband or wife in this season. Not what man say, but what God has approved for your life and destiny in Christ. God gives us what He thinks is best for us. What is best for us is sometimes not what we want!

But it is what God say we need and is good for us.

Answer the call God place on your life, it's unique, it's distinct, it is for a set people, place and time! Don't judge your call by man's opinion. Don't allow your environment to dictate your purpose! Be like Noah, and ***"Dare To Be Bold"*** even in the midst of ridicule, mockery and criticism. Obey God and accept His divine plan for your life! It may not be a call like what is so familiar in the kingdom! It is unique God says! Say **'YES'** to the Lord, and He will instruct you and teach you and guide you into your promise!

Where He leads you to connect and fellowship in this season is for you to complete or finish your course for the purpose and assignment on your life! It may not feel like the traditional church or ministry but position yourself to serve that leader and watch God.

Is it likely that, you're in position for the Lord to say to you ***"You have found favor in my eyes?"*** God expects us as His children to stand for what is right, even when everyone else may insist you are wrong. My advice to you is, obey God and confidently declare that:-

"I AM ANOINTED FOR THIS"!

Chapter 2

Seeing the Light

Matthew 5:13-15 [KJV] ***"Ye are the salt of the earth: but if the salt have lost his savor, wherewith shall it be salted? It is thenceforth good for nothing, but to be cast out, and to be trodden under foot of men. 14 Ye are the light of the world. A city that is set on a hill cannot be hid. 15 Neither do men light a candle, and put it under a bushel, but on a candlestick; and it giveth light unto all that are in the house."***

In this chapter we will view a synopsis of Paul's life to reveal how God used even adverse experiences in life to prepare us to boldly stand with confidence saying, ***"I AM ANOINTED FOR THIS."***

Paul laid out his life transparent in a series of epistles to the early church that make up much of what we recognize today as the New Testament.

We first meet Paul as Saul, which was his name before he became transformed into a believer of Jesus Christ. His persecution of those who believed in Jesus as the Messiah is first mentioned in Acts chapter one and verse eight [1:8]. Saul was involved in the stoning death of Stephen, the first martyr of the Christian faith. Saul's miraculous conversion to Paul took place on the road to Damascus.

A startling light from heaven flashed around him. He fell to the ground and heard a voice say to him, ***"Saul, Saul, why do you persecute me?" "Who are you Lord?' Saul asked. "I am Jesus, whom you are persecuting,"*** He replied [Acts 9:3-5]. From that moment on Paul' began ***"Seeing the Light"***.

This transformation positioned Paul into <u>one of the Greatest Evangelist who never limits the message</u>. He went about preaching the gospel of Jesus in season and out of season regardless of the obstacles, trials, hardship or persecution he had to endure or confront. Paul's life was re-directed, re-instituted, re-vitalized by the Spirit's Power, who anointed him for a great work. What he was prior, was no longer after his transformation process.

He was a persecutor of the church, on the road to Damascus to do more damage to the church, killing and persecuting the saints.

But God, had a plan to take over every avenue of his life. Saul transformation to Paul took place as he heeded the instructions given to him by the Lord after blinding his eyes for three (3) days. Can I tell you something the devil can't do more than his time allotted to him by the boss. His boss is Jesus. The adversary the devil only have access that God himself gave him and what you will also allow. Are you hearing me clearly, but when God gets ready, every demonic powers, every satanic squatters, every diabolical assignment and plots will be annihilated.

So Paul could attest that ***"I Am Anointed For This"*** with these words, ***"My old self has been crucified with Christ. It is no longer I who live, but Christ lives in me. So I live in this earthly body by trusting in the Son of God, who loved me and gave himself for me"*** [Galatians 2:19-20 - NLT].
"I have been crucified with Christ. It is no longer I who live, but Christ who lives in me. And the life I now live in the flesh I live by

faith in the Son of God, who loved me and gave himself for me" [Galatians 2:19-20 – ESV].

When you suffer for Christ you shall reign with Him. It is the cross [trials, tests] we have to bear that proves us and position us with ***"Fireproof Faith"*** to declare, ***"I Am Anointed For This."*** *'The 'Glory is in the Story.'* Everybody wants the 'Glory', but not everyone willing to pay the price for the 'Glory' [The anointing]. The anointing is marked by suffering, persecution and trial.

1 Peter 1:7-9 declares:-

> ***"Pure gold put in the fire comes out of it proved pure; genuine faith put through this suffering comes out proved genuine. When Jesus wraps this all up, it's your faith, not your gold, that God will have on display as evidence of his victory. 8 You never saw him, yet you love him. You still don't see him, yet you trust him - with laughter and singing. 9 Because you kept on believing, you'll get what you're looking forward to: total salvation."***

The anointing comes with a price or cost. It cost you sacrifice, suffering, persecution, and trials. You have to go through the process for God to trust you with greatness. If you look up the definition of "GREATNESS":- Greatness comes with great sacrifice as well as rewards. To say that, ***"I Am Anointed For This"*** is a declaration that, *'I have been tested and tried and God has proven my faith to be genuine!'* Then God lavishes you with unsurmountable wealth and victories unstoppable, even in the areas that seem like a desert and a wilderness you will flourish and it will marvel those who persecute you, plot against you and tried to kill you. Remember this as Paul declares in:-

> Galatians 2:19-20, ***"My old self has been crucified with Christ. It is no longer I who live, but Christ lives in me. So I live in this earthly body by trusting in the Son of God who loved me and gave himself for me."***

"I AM ANOINTED FOR THIS."
Simply put: - **I AM ANOINTED FOR THIS! And I CAN DO ALL THINGS THROUGH CHRIST WHO STRENGTHENS ME!**

Chapter 3

God Can Reach Anyone

Paul's life was transformed into a ministry of gratitude, depicting God's mercy and grace. Through Jesus Christ, every single person on the earth can have a second chance just like Paul, or even a third, or fourth. Reading Paul story will excite you to be passionate about serving the Lord. His story is one of massive reconstruction.

The transformation was very great from his participation in the stoning death of Stephen, the first Christian martyr to his legacy as a powerful Evangelist for Christ. Part of Paul's transformation had to do with Ananias praying for his deliverance and a transference of the anointing for the assignment that took place.

I can testify that, someone had to be praying for me. I was on the road to a devil's hell and God blocked it with the prayer of my mother, my high school teacher, Amoy Rhoe, who was also a member of the church I attended. Thanking God for the prayers of Mrs. Amoy Rhoe, The late Rev. Eulalee Robinson, and Deaconess Wilson in particular. I know others may have prayed but these people would send messages home of encouragement that they missed me and they were praying for me.

You can attest as well that someone prayed you back on track because they saw the uniqueness of what the Lord wanted to do in your life. God gave them spiritual insight into your destiny and they began to call it forth through intercession. I would wake up every morning with olive oil over on my forehead each morning and a Bible track on top of my chest drawer in my room, as my Mother watched over us [my sisters and myself] in prayer while we sleep.

When the Lord spoke to Ananias of His intentions to deliver Saul and use him for His glory, initially, Ananias was hesitant, knowing what Saul was heading to Damascus to execute. Saul had a "Missionary spirit" with the wrong perspective, attitude and motive. Saul was not content to punish some and to drive the rest from the "holy city." He did not want to merely contain Christianity or to drive it from Jerusalem; he wanted to rid the earth of Christianity and its followers.

Thus, his opposition to Christ and His church took on a "missionary" spirit. Saul went to other cities where he sought to arrest Christians and to bring them back to Jerusalem for punishment. Damascus, a city some 150 miles to the northeast of Jerusalem, was one such city. Word was out that Saul would soon be arriving.

On his way to Damascus, Saul was struck by a bright light from heaven, symbolizing God's Spirit, power and presence. When he arose, he was blind and was instructed by God to enter the city and then he will be told what to do. Some of us, will be literally struck by God with some stormy trials just for us to come in alignment with His will. Saul who became Paul, was without sight for three (3) days, neither did he eat nor drink. God spoke to Ananias about his plan of transformation <u>from Saul to Paul</u>.

> ***"And there was a certain disciple at Damascus, named Ananias; and to him said the Lord in a vision, Ananias. And he said, Behold, I am here, Lord.11 And the Lord said unto him, Arise, and go into***

the street which is called Straight, and enquire in the house of Judas for one called Saul, of Tarsus: for,

behold, he prayeth, 12 And hath seen in a vision a man named Ananias coming in, and putting his hand on him, that he might receive his sight. 13 Then Ananias answered, Lord, I have heard by many of this man, how much evil he hath done to thy saints at Jerusalem: 14 And here he hath authority from the chief priests to bind all that call on thy name. 15 But the Lord said unto him, Go thy way: for he is a chosen vessel unto me, to bear my name before the Gentiles, and kings, and the children of Israel: 16 For I will shew him how great things he must suffer for my name's sake. 17 And Ananias went his way, and entered into the house; and putting his hands on him said, Brother Saul, the Lord, even Jesus, that appeared unto thee in the way as thou camest, hath sent me, that thou mightest receive thy sight, and be filled with the Holy Ghost. 18 And immediately there fell from his eyes as it had been scales: and he received sight forthwith, and arose, and was

baptized. 19 And when he had received meat, he was strengthened. Then was Saul certain days with the disciples which were at Damascus. 20 And straightway he preached Christ in the synagogues, that he is the Son of God. 21 But all that heard him were amazed, and said; Is not this he that destroyed them which called on this name in Jerusalem, and came hither for that intent, that he might bring them bound unto the chief priests?"22 But Saul increased the more in strength, and confounded the Jews which dwelt at Damascus, proving that this is very Christ" [Acts 9:10-22].

Many times people over look us because of our past mistakes and what they know about us previously. But God already was dealing with Saul before entering Damascus. Ananias had to perform God's divine wish to release Paul to the work. We all can identify with our past sin or mistakes and how and when the transition and transformation took place. We had to deal with people who knew about our life story and issues we had before we got saved. We had to stay the course and let your light shine so the world could see the transformation.

> ***"Then Ananias answered, Lord, I have heard by many of this man, how much evil he hath done to thy saints at Jerusalem: 14 And here he hath authority from the chief priests to bind all that call on thy name. 15 But the Lord said unto him, Go thy way: for he is a chosen vessel unto me, to bear my name before the Gentiles, and kings, and the children of Israel"***
> [Acts 9:13-15].

I don't know the hell you have been through by the hands of your persecutors or the things you have done in your life that you may have regretted or feel ashamed of. Take a note from Paul's life and inject into yours that, **'God can take a mess and make it a message.'** Satan cannot kill what God permits to live. Your sons, daughters or your husband may have gone wayward, but trust the Holy Spirit and the power of God's word in you to speak faith and life into a dead situation.

"And Ananias went his way, and entered into the house; and putting his hands on him said, Brother Saul, the Lord, even Jesus, that appeared unto thee in the way as thou camest, hath sent me, that thou mightest receive thy sight, and be filled with the Holy Ghost. 18 And immediately there fell from his eyes as it had been scales: and he received sight forthwith, and arose, and was baptized. 19 And when he had received meat, he was strengthened. Then was Saul certain days with the disciples which were at Damascus. 20 And straightway he preached Christ in the synagogues, that he is the Son of God. 21 But all that heard him were amazed, and said; Is not this he that destroyed them which called on this name in Jerusalem, and came hither for that intent, that he might bring them bound unto the chief priests?"

There is no sin too deep that God can't reach us. No matter where we go, God can bring us back to where we should be in Him and use us for His glory in a mighty way. Like Paul, no matter what sins we've committed, no matter what story our past has to tell, we are brand new when we come to know Jesus Christ. Paul's life is a shining example of all God can do when we are willing to give ourselves and others another chance.

Declare it right now over yourself and someone you have been praying for to be delivered that ________________ is **"Anointed for This."**
Remember that, God not only uses victory but also adversities to bring us closer to our destiny.

Chapter 4

You Have What It Takes

Acts 9:15 ***"But the Lord said to him, "Go, for he is a chosen vessel of Mine to bear My name before Gentiles, kings, and the children of Israel."***

God chose Paul to take the message of Jesus Christ to all people. He also gave him everything he needed to accomplish his purpose. I dare you to tell yourself as well as call three (3) people and tell them **'nothing that happens in your life will be wasted, you are chosen by God to a great assignment.'** Saul was a well learnt man. You may not be Saul transformed into a Paul, but you have your story to tell. You have some tests that has and will become a testimony.

You probably have a past that the enemy is using to torment you, but today it is over. God desires to use you. Whether you were suicidal, struck out on drugs, or alcohol, battling anxiety and or depression. Maybe you were living or now living a care-free life of partying and sexual promiscuity or just a rebellious old soul. God can and will use that to transform someone's life if you surrender to His will and let Him have his way in your life. Through the transformation from the old adamic nature to a new life in Christ you will be able to tell somebody that, *'The blood of Jesus cleanse me, the blood of Jesus changed me, and the blood of Jesus has miraculous power.'*

You may have grown up in Sunday school, was in church for most of your youthful days and went wayward. You know what! You probably in the church doing the worldly stuff on the side but God sees something great in you that can be cultivated if you let Him. All you need to do is surrender to His will.

"I am the true grapevine, and my Father is the gardener. 2 He cuts off every branch of mine that doesn't produce fruit, and he prunes the branches that do bear fruit so they will produce even more. 3 You have already been pruned and purified by the message I have given you.

4 Remain in me, and I will remain in you. For a branch cannot produce fruit if it is severed from the vine, and you cannot be fruitful unless you remain in me. 5 "Yes, I am the vine; you are the branches. Those who remain in me, and I in them, will produce much fruit. For apart from me you can do nothing. 6 Anyone who does not remain in me is thrown away like a useless branch and withers. Such branches are gathered into a pile to be burned. 7 But if you remain in me and my words remain in you, you may ask for anything you want, and it will be granted! 8 When you produce much fruit, you are my true disciples. This brings great glory to my Father."
[St. John 15:1-8, NLT].

You have what it takes, all you need to do is yield yourself completely to the Lord. Abide in Him and let His word abide in you. The word of God embedded in your heart will prune you and purify you and cause you to become fruitful and more fruitful as you continually and constantly abide in Him. If you trust Him to take over every area of your life, He will cut off, root up, and pluck up that which does not produce fruit in your life, and prune that which has potential in your life to manifest more fruitfulness **"You Have What It Takes**!" Say it loud, ***"I AM ANOINTED FOR THIS"***!

Many reading this right now, may have strayed from the faith or feel like you want to give up on the dream or vision God gave you. You feel like a failure or may feel like He cannot use you anymore. Prior to Paul's conversion into Christianity, his Hebrew name was Saul. He was a Pharisee, strictly trained in the law and Jewish traditions, fluent in Hebrew, Greek, and Aramaic, so he could communicate well with many people. God used that knowledge and experience gained after his transformation

Whatever, you surrender to God, he is able to transform it and use it for His Glory. The message is already imprinted in your heart from Sunday school, through your Pastors, the Prophets and Evangelist that poured into your life. Even the words of instruction you had ignored that came directly from the Lord to you.

At the moment you may feel like you are backed up in a corner. I can hear you in the spirit lamenting before God. I am also speaking to Five-Fold Ministers, Worshippers, and Prayer Warriors, and those on the forefront or frontline in ministry who have gone through some upheaval in ministry and wondering what in the world went on here. It seems like a tsunami has hit your life, or ministry.

Your family life appears chaotic, children and or church folk getting to your nerves! Hold out and hold on my brothers and my sisters, let me give you a sneak peak of what is about to happen in your life.

The Lord says: - ***'Trust me, you have what it takes. What is about to happen – NEXT -will be greater than your struggles. There will be a cataclysmic explosion of My power in your heart and into your life.'* Shout Next is Greater** !!!

At the worst point in Paul's life, blinded, and could not see where he was going, was his tipping point for his transformation. For a while, he thought he had all the "I's" dotted and the "T's" crossed, but God showed him through a divine visitation that it was time for a takeover.

It is time to let go and let God, you have done your part of trying to fix things, and trying to help God. He doesn't need your help in this season. You have done the best you could in a bad situation. In addition to that, you tried your best to keep focus in spite of all the distractions but it seems like you still can't keep it together in the family or the ministry.

Right now, this very moment, God is taking you on a new journey. A new level of seeking, restoration, transformation for elevation and promotion in this season. You may have been counted out by many who looked down upon you because you choose a different path. You chose to separate yourself from folly. Well, the revelation of Jesus Christ is getting ready to explode in your heart. God is ready to unveil and provide the most important thing you need for the next level of the journey and walk of faith for the new season and dimension He is taking you into.

I feel the shift right now taking place in my atmosphere as I write this prophetically to you:-

The Lord is re-directing and re-ordering your steps. He is removing some

persons, habits and things from your life for a greater explosion of His power in your life. This release or greater explosion of power is for where the Lord is about to take you spiritually, in ministry, as well for the new places you are about to travel. Not to mention the new connections He is trying to bring into your life.'

You should be dancing right now, it is working for your good! God is trying to get everything in your life in this season to conform to His will. No time for foolish people and foolish conversation. No need to be indecisive about the move that's on in your life right now. He is getting you deeper in sync with the anointing to fulfill your God-given mission, to say and do with greater precision just what the Father intended.

For Paul, the revelation of Jesus Christ exploded in his heart and provided the most important thing he needed to become all that God destined him to be. God is doing that, right now in your life:-

'The revelation of Jesus Christ is exploding into your heart and providing the most important thing you

needed to become all that God destined you to be.'

Refuse the lie that you don't have what it takes. Everything it takes to do what God destined you to do is already within you through the power of Christ Jesus. Say it out loud: - ***"I AM ANOINTED FOR THIS!"***

Chapter 5

Your Season of Waiting

It is in your season of waiting that God anoints you. Isaiah's 40:31 declares that

"But those who trust in the Lord will find new strength. They will soar high on wings like eagles. They will run and not grow weary. They will walk and not faint."

There is a period of testing, trials, and re-positioning that takes place in your life that prepares you for what God wants you to do or prepares you for the blessings He has for you. Many times we tend to gravitate towards "Anointed" men and women of the Gospel because of what they carry. We are drawn to them because of the demonstration of the power of God in their lives.

I can recall personally, several times I prayed that God would anoint me like Pastor Jackie McCullough when I was a babe in Christ. Then I realize that what I was praying for, was not only the anointing on her life, but the tests, trials and or processes that comes with cultivating the anointing Pastor Jackie McCullough carries.

In addition to that, I was placing limitations on the power of God available to me. Remember that the word is sure, God honors His word above His name and He remind us that, ***"Now to Him who is able to do exceedingly, abundantly above all that we ask or think, according to the power that works in us"*** [Ephesians 3:20]. Praying for someone else's anointing, would defeat God's unique purpose and ability to emerge through you. Understand that it is in the furnace of affliction that God will try you, prune you and build you for *"A Great and High Destiny*!"

Let me re-emphasize this: - Praying for someone else's anointing, would defeat God's unique purpose and ability to emerge through you. Understand that it is the trials by fire, persecution, life circumstances through which God will try you, prune you build you and approve you for *"A Great and High Destiny"*! Let us end this year with intense prayer and praise and worship, knowing that He will give us the desires our heart. Let us expect more, and ask for more, demonstrating residual courage because of what Christ has already done for our souls on the cross.

Even as I write this, *'the Spirit of Lord is speaking to me to tell you, you are about to walk into a new season and you are "**[I Am] Anointed for This**"*. **"This"** represents your future assignment. It represents, also new trials or obstacles that you might face as a challenge to enter into your new season.

Yes, you got that right. You will face similar Devils, same tricks but if you mastered the strategies God gave you in that season of waiting, [I believe you have and will master them]. The anointing derived from your obedience during that period, is what qualifies you to withstand the "Wiles of the Devil" in your new season. You are ***"Anointed for This."***

This is your season, this is your time. Remember grapes are crushed so the juice can run out.

➢ Your endurance is being admired.

➢ Your integrity is being mentioned in circles that you would least expect or dream of.

In your season of waiting, the Lord is positioning you for *"Greatness With Fireproof Faith!"*

> ➢ The rejection you experienced during your waiting period is just a door, not a wall.
> ➢ When you remain determined and persistent in your season of waiting and pursuit after your destiny, it will attract people of worth that will cause you to achieve in a single day what would normally require a year for you to achieve.
> ➢ While you are waiting in His presence, the Lord is doing what seems impossible **SUDDENLY!**

Your Season of Waiting

Prophetic Prayer Declaration

Lord I thank you for the people, places and things you are about to bring into my life. Thank you Lord that, my faith is focus-driven and focus-driven is being purpose-driven. I decree and declare that being purpose-driven is a vehicle derived from being faith-focus that drives and propels me into my future and destiny.

Thank you for the grace and tenacity to stay the course. I decree and declare that my tenacity is attracting attention of the right people to me. I decree and declare, "I Am Anointed For This" and I will not abort my purpose because destiny is calling me. Lord, I thank you that my tenacity, like Hannah is attracting the right people to me and has placed a demand on heaven.

I decree and declare that my diligence is paying off right NOW – SUDDENLY! I shall stand before kings, I shall not stand before mean men according to Proverbs 22:29.

I decree and declare that the right people according to your divine will and plan for my life is seeking to connect with me and asking about me for the right reason and will not deter me but improve my vision and propel my destiny. I decree and declare that when these people enter my life, I will achieve in a single day suddenly what would normally require a year for me to accomplish alone in Jesus name! "I AM ANOINTED FOR THIS"

Chapter 6

The Refiner's Fire

"God has a way of releasing His Glory in your life" [T.D. Jakes]. The greater the trials you experience, the greater the anointing you will receive.

"For our light affliction, which is but for a moment, worketh for us a far more exceeding and eternal weight of glory" [2 Corinthians 4:17]

In your season of waiting the Lord uses the afflictions you experience to refine you for greater, or a new beginning [fresh start]. The New Living translation explains that,

"17 For our present troubles are small and won't last very long. Yet they produce for us a glory that vastly outweighs them and will last forever! 18 So we don't look at the troubles we can see now; rather, we fix our gaze on things that cannot be seen."

The refinement process reveals God heart towards us, desiring us to become increasingly more effective, elegant [a spirit of excellence].You find strength to endure the refining process by focusing on the promises of God. Looking at what your end is going to be, increases your tenacity as you wait on the Lord.

Refine also means to reduce to a pure state. John 3:30 says ***"He must increase, but I must decrease"***. Increase represents growth, upsurge or arise. After this! There will be an upsurge of God's glory in your life. Hold on a little while longer. In removing unwanted material from our lives [refiner's fire] we are fit for the Masters use.

The Refining Process

As we are purified by God, His reflection in our lives will become more and more clear to those around us. God says that the Levites (Israel leaders) should be especially open to his purification process in their lives.

"But ye are a chosen generation. A royal priesthood, a holy nation, a peculiar people; that ye should shew forth the praises of him who hath called you out of darkness into his marvelous light."
[1 Peter 2:9].

In the process of refining metals, the raw metal is heated with fire until it melts. The impurities separate from it and rise to the surface. They are skimmed off leaving the pure metal. Without this heating and melting, there could be no purifying. **God's presence is guaranteed in the refining process.** You are being purified for purpose and He is with you during the process.

As the impurities are skimmed off the top, the reflection of the worker appears in the clear, pure surface. That means God wants to be the reflection in our lives, one of excellence and high standard. For us to become increasingly more effective, elegant [a spirit of excellence] there is a price to pay. Your trials seem like they are over taking you on every side, but in the midst of all that, the one thing the Lord demands is your brokenness.

As you endure the refining process, the reflection of the Holy Spirit appears and is evident and visible in your life and ministry. Brokenness is an indication that you are ***"Anointed For This."*** That is, your next assignment, breakthrough or blessing.

David was overtaken by trials, attacks and enemies on every side, but yet still he said in Psalm 27:3-4 that,

> ***"Though a host should encamp against me, my heart shall not fear: though war should rise against me, in this will I be confident. 4 One thing have I desired of the Lord, that will I seek after; that I may dwell in the house of the Lord all the days of my life, to behold the beauty of the Lord, and to enquire in his temple."***

Your brokenness [evidence of repentance] is found in the fruit of your faith. Your brokenness before God shows evidence of your dependence on Him. A large enemy battle was positioned to do battle against David. Still, David choose to seek the face of the Lord, even with such great odds against him.

David declared: - *"I CHOOSE TO WORSHIP."* David choose to praise and worship the Lord, shifting the atmosphere for miracles and breakthroughs, that could not possible be attained in the natural surrounded by enemy forces.

When you worship God in the midst of the fire, it makes the process stress-free because worship releases inner peace and outwardly create an atmosphere for God to re-direct and annihilate the attack of the enemy. Understand this, that what you need is on the other side of the GLORY. The trial, attacks of the enemy, bitter season or storm is a detractor from the greater release, breakthrough, blessing and power that awaits you beyond the veil.

Worship catapult you into the supernatural. Take a lesson from David's life, the life of Job and not to mention three (3) Hebrew Boys. These legendary leaders of faith choose to worship the Lord with confidence because there was a fourth man in the fire. His name is Jesus. The test, the trials or adversity is meant to refine you.

Refine means to improve (something) by making small changes, in particular make (an idea, theory, or method) more subtle and accurate. The refiners fire, removes impurities or unwanted elements from (a substance) typically as part of an industrial [SPIRITUAL] process: Sugar was refined by boiling it in huge vats.

In the process of refining metals, the raw metal is heated with fire until it melts. The goldsmith sits over the gold, and never leave. He sees the process into completion. Likewise, God will never leave you in your moment of weakness, or place of limitation and brokenness. 2 Corinthians 12:8-10 says:-

> *"For this thing I besought the Lord thrice, that it might depart from me. 9 And he said unto me, My grace is sufficient for thee: for my strength is made perfect in weakness. Most gladly therefore will I rather glory in my infirmities, that the power of Christ may rest upon me. 10 Therefore I take pleasure in infirmities, in reproaches, in necessities, in persecutions, in distresses for Christ's sake: for when I am weak, then am I strong."*

The goldsmith sits there over the gold. He watches and work with the gold as the impurities separate from it and rise to the surface. The impurities are then skimmed off leaving the pure metal. The anointing will be distinct on your live because you have yielded yourself to the process, identifying with the sufferings of Christ, and embracing the power of Christ through His grace.

Without this heating and melting, there will be no purifying. As the impurities are skimmed off the top, the reflection of the worker appears in the clear, pure surface. Without the heating and melting work of the Holy Spirit in our lives, their will be no manifest evidence of the power of the Lord Jesus in our lives. While we wait in His presence, Jesus the Master Potter reshapes us, and transforms us into a vessel fit for the Master's use. God is preparing you for increase. The refining process positions you for an upgrade which is same as increase. Increase meaning growth, to arise, or an upsurge.

God says ***"Tell my people that they are in a season of Increase!"*** If you find yourself going through the refining process, you are being ***"Redefined"*** for a season of explosion of God's supernatural increase and favor.

Ecclesiastes 1:18 ***"The greater my wisdom, the greater the grief. To increase knowledge only increase sorrow"***.

Ezekiel 36:11 ***"I will increase not only the people, but also your animals. O mountain of Israel, I will bring people to live once again. I will even make you more prosperous than you were before. Then you will know that I am the Lord."***

Lord, I thank you that I am being redefined and repositioned for an upgrade. I decree and declare, and say thank you that I am ***"Positioned for an Upgrade" and "I Am Anointed for This."***

I can recall in my earlier Christian walk I was under so much pressure from every side. All my friends were gone, separated because of my new walk in Christ. I was in church and felt lonely because, I was always worshipping and weeping at the same time and nobody understood me. Some rejected me or just avoided me because they thought I was different or overreacting. In the midst of that I was experiencing severe spiritual warfare in my sleep and while awake from demonic attacks.

The attacks were constant against my body and my mind. At one point the enemy told me to kill myself. But I looked in the mirror and talked back to myself and said, I shall not die but live. I said devil you should have killed me before I was born. As a matter a fact, I said devil, it's too late now because now I am born again. I was experiencing a series of battle fatigue from constantly praying and warfaring. I kept reminding myself of God's promises in the scriptures that I memorized daily with confidence that, ***"Greater is He that is in me than he that is in the world."***

Another scripture I generally quoted was, ***"Being confident in this very thing that He that hath begun a good work in you is able to complete it until the day of Jesus Christ"*** [Philippians 1:6].

Then in the midst of that happening in my mind, I heard the divine instruction from the Lord that has carried me to this day and made me into a Prophetic Worshipping Warrior of Jesus Christ and prepared: - [*"Anointed Me for This"*] season doing Kingdom Business for the Lord.

The Lord spoke to me:- He said, *"Daughter, I know you love me and desire to worship me in Spirit and in truth."* I said yes Lord. *"Here is what I need you to do; constantly praise me, this will counter and defeat the attacks of the enemy against your life.* I said yes Lord. He said, *"Daughter, the only way to conquer these attacks is through worship, you have no other option than to praise your way through. I want you to praise me constantly everyday".* The Lord further clarified how to worship. He said, *"Worship me with Psalm, hymn and spiritual song as well as worshipping in the Spirt"* [Worshipping in tongues].

You can interview my mother and my father and siblings if you like, they will verify that, I worshipped none stop, all day and all night. I remember several times my dad would stop home during the day from operating his taxi-cab and find me worshipping still after 1:00 p.m. He would sometimes come later at 3:00 p.m. to see if it is still the same and it was, I was still worshipping. I couldn't explain it to them, because then I thought they wouldn't understand and I did not want my mother to worry.

After several years, [3-4 years] battle of intense warfare, I overcame, just less than two years before migrating to the United States. I got the victory and had risen to a greater level of spiritual maturity knowing who I was and the authority [Exousia] I had in Him.

It was after that test, that the Lord opened the door to teach at a local bible college by Pastor Clementson Smith on the topic: - **"Prophetic in Warfare"** in Jamaica. How it happened can only be described as "The Suddenlies of God." I graduated Bible College in August 2000, and two weeks after graduation, suddenly I received a phone call from her that the Lord told her I should teach on that topic at her college. I said are you sure because, I don't have the experience that you need. Maybe Bishop Norman Lewin or Bishop Courtney McLean would do a better job, I said, they have more experience. At the time I was a member of the group called, the "Remnant Ministries International" and they were the Presidents so I recommended them.

She refuted my suggestions and insisted that the Lord spoke to her concerning me. *"Furthermore, I won't be telling you what to teach, nor the strategies to use in teaching teach the course."* Yes, the Lord says *you are the one he has chosen to teach, and He will reveal to you the outline."* The Lord instructed me as to the strategy for the course and for every class there was a powerful move of God, coupled with teaching each week.

God knew **"I Was Anointed For This"** [The assignment to teach]. No test or trial you endure will go wasted. I thought, it was too intensifying the warfare for a babe in Christ, only three (3) months into my salvation [conversion] at the time. Not to mention, immediately after my baptism that night it seemed like all hell broke loose. But God had a plan, one that could not be stopped or blocked. The onus was on me to trust God and walk it out by faith.

Will you succumb to the pressures of the tests or afflictions, our will the Lord find the fruit of your faith as evidence of your perseverance? Even with such great odds against him, David's confidence in God speaks volume that, **"I Am Anointed For This."** David's declaration in Psalm 27:3 says,

"When the armies of the enemy surround me, I will not be afraid. When death calls for me in the midst of war, my soul is confident and unmoved."

Simply put, *"My confidence remained unshakable in God."* It is in our moments of weakness that allows the glory of the Lord to be revealed.

"We are troubled on every side, yet not distressed; we are perplexed, but not in despair; 9 persecuted, but not forsaken; cast down, but not destroyed; 10 always bearing about in the body the dying of the Lord Jesus that the life also of Jesus might be made manifest in our body" [2 Corinthians 4:8-10]. *"For this thing I besought the Lord thrice, that it might depart from me. 9 And he said unto me, My grace is sufficient for thee: for my strength is made perfect in weakness." Most gladly therefore will I rather glory in my infirmities, that the power of Christ may rest upon me."*
[2 Corinthians 12:8-9].

Even though, God did not remove Paul's affliction, He promised to demonstrate His power in Paul. We see throughout the Epistles the account of Paul's life and the power of God demonstrated not only to proclaim the gospel with signs and wonders, but also how God delivered him from danger and shackles.

Paul wanted to increase his power by the removal of the "thorn." God showed him where his true sufficiency was. Power came through seeing weakness as the very vehicle for manifesting the power of Christ, not through gradually removing the problem or weakness. I hope you get this, it is through your trials by fire that the anointing emerge or manifest.

Weakness shows the inadequacy of the vessel and affirm the ever-present grace and power of the Spirit within.

2 Corinthians 4:7 declares, ***"7 But we have this treasure in earthen vessels, that the excellency of the power may be of God, and not of us."***

In the refining process, it is describes as a process of removal whereby God is making us free from any coarse, unsuitable, or immoral characteristics. Anything that may tarnish our reputation and integrity and in turn scar our ministry and have a negative effect on the body of Christ. The refining process is freeing us from impurities, allowing us to become polished and elegant. God uses His Holy Spirit to perform precise peculiarities and refinement in our thoughts and speech as He burns within us.

If you don't allow God to finish this process in you, then your ministry will obviously become short lived and your divine purpose and will become watered done to traditions of men and religious norms, lacking the power or dunamis of God. We have the assurance through His word that God will make His power known in our circumstances. You should boldly declare that, ***"I Am Anointed For This."***

Knowing that God's power is displayed in our weaknesses, should give us courage and hope. Knowing that we have to depend on His power, helps us to recognize our limitations as a result we will depend on God more for our effectiveness rather than on our own energy, effort, or talent. Our human limitations not only help us develop Christian character but also deepen our worship and seek after God. In admitting our human limitations we affirm God's strength. In so doing, when He begins to use us mightily, God gets all the glory, that you are *'Anointed for This.'*

Positioned for an Upgrade

God is positioning you for an *'Upgrade.'* He will use that test or trial to promote you and shift you into a new dimension of His power that His name be glorified. The test, trials and storms are all a part of the process of refining you. Refine: means to, enhance, cultivate or upgrade.

Upgrade means to raise the standard, to raise to a higher grade! It means improving or progressing. If God is preparing you for an upgrade then it takes time. During your season of waiting God is preparing you for greater.

David did not recognize that he was positioned for an upgrade while tending to his father, Jesse's sheep. I feel like David, with the experience I shared earlier in the chapter. He went through intense warfare while tending to the sheep, warding off and fighting lions and bears. Not only that, his brothers had the privilege to go to battle as soldiers against the Philistines, while he had to tend to the sheep's and goats.

But step by step God divinely ordered David's life. Can I tell you, step by step God has ordered your life? David was the son his father had forgotten.

But on the back side of the desert, the preparation and ***"Refiners Fire"*** process began for an upgrade. His own father did not see his 'KINGLY' potential. Samuel was strategically and diplomatically sent by God to Jesse's house to find the next king. David was left out on the back side with the sheep while his brothers one by one paraded before Samuel for selection.

All seven sons came before Samuel but they were not God's choice.

"But Samuel said to Jesse, "The Lord has not chosen any of these." 11 Then Samuel asked, "Are these all the sons you have?" "There is still the youngest," Jesse replied. "But he's out in the fields watching the sheep and goats. Send for him at once, Samuel said. We will not sit down to eat until he arrives."12 So Jesse sent for him. He was dark and handsome, with beautiful eyes. And the Lord said, "This is the one; anoint him."

This scene in the chapter brings to the light that waiting patiently before the Lord and be anxious for nothing mentality, regardless of the obstacles placed before you will bring forth a sweet victory and end.

> ***"Blessed are those who endure when they are tested. When they pass the test, they will receive the crown of life that God has promised to those who love him"*** [James 1:12].

Oh yes, there was one, positioned for an upgrade out of clear view. He was in hiding until his set time. Don't see rejection as just pain. It is for your protection that God separated you, because what is coming 'NEXT' in your life is greater. SHOUT IT LOUD! ***"NEXT IS GREATER!"*** Hallelujah, give the Lord praise.

While those around you think you don't have what it takes, God sees your heart. David's father did not see any potential in him, yet God saw his heart instead of his appearance and called David to lead His chosen people.

"I've searched the land and found this David, son of Jesse. He's a man whose heart beats to my heart, a man who will do what I tell him" [Acts 13:22b].

God is moving with a spiritual radar looking for the next David to anoint! Declare it, **"I Am Anointed For This!"** It is just a test. God has positioned you for an upgrade. It is a **'Kingly Anointing'** that will and can stand against the giants [Goliaths] that dare to mock the God in you.

Greatness takes time. Greatness is not instantaneous it takes endurance, perseverance and persistence. After which success will come step by step and God will drive out [remove] the hindrances along the way. Exodus 23:29-30 says:-

"But I will not drive them out in a single year, because the land would become desolate and the wild animals would multiply and threaten you.

30 I will drive them out a little at a time until your population has increased enough to take possession of the land".

Not all the time God's solution is instantaneous. Nor delay justify inaction. All He ask for in the refining process is your cooperation. Constant cooperation and persistency is all God asked from the Israelites. But as they progressed through their journey in the wilderness things got uglier and they began to murmur and complain. If things seem to be getting dreadful or you have just passed through some unpleasant, bitter wilderness season then God is preparing you for promotion [**An upgrade**].

The refining process reveals that all the impurities rise to the top. This means it takes time to enter into greatness because, as described by the history of the text, wild beast and wild animals would have to be removed from the land, so they don't have no settled area where God was taking them. These wild beast and or animals represent foreign settlers [squatters] who served other God's, and are not a worshipper of Jehovah.

God will drive out and remove any hindrances to your destiny.

To keep it real, there are people that the Lord will separate you from because they have no connection to where you are going or have no understanding of your purpose and assignment. They don't know and comprehend the realms of worship that God is elevating you to. That is why you must separate yourself. The refining process calls for separation.

> Ex. 23:32-33 ***"You will make no covenant with them, nor with their gods. They shall not dwell in your land, lest they make you sin against me. For if you serve their gods, it will surely be a snare to you"***.

The refining process removes the squatters from your life as God aligns you with people of like mind and spirit who connects to you in order to help you or show you kindness. As a result of this divine connection it propels you into your area or position of GREATNESS. The refiner's fire remove the impurities, therefore it also remove unwanted, non-productive, vain worshippers, people who doesn't uphold the standard of holiness and righteousness in your life.

They don't understand your change of heart and worship, they are quick to judge and criticize you. They call you out your name, **"When did you become so anointed."** Sounds familiar doesn't it?

They form clicks to talk about the old you! But I double dare you to speak it out loud, *'I'm a new creation, old things are passed away, BEHOLD, all things are made new.'* "It doesn't take all that!" they say. Oh, yes it does! Ask the '*Women at the Well'* in St. John 4. God's getting ready to remove some folks [drama] out of your life so that your increase can come forth! Declare it today, **"I Am Positioned For An Upgrade"** and **"I Am Anointed For This."**

> John 15:1-7 **"I am the true vine, and My Father is the vinedresser. 2 Every branch in Me that does not bear fruit He takes away; and every branch that bears fruit He prunes, that it may bear more fruit. 3 You are already clean because of the word which I have spoken to you. 4 Abide in Me, and I in you. As the branch cannot bear fruit of**

itself, unless it abides in the vine, neither can you, unless you abide in Me. 5 "I am the vine, you are the branches. He who abides in Me, and I in him, bears much fruit; for without Me you can do nothing. 6 If anyone does not abide in Me, he is cast out as a branch and is withered; and they gather them and throw them into the fire, and they are burned. 7 If you abide in Me, and My words abide in you, you will ask what you desire, and it shall be done for you"

He is raising you up! You who were exiled, who have been through the refining process, as well as persevered continuously and constantly, through the process. This process enables you to teach others "true worship".

It takes "TRUE WORSHIP" which comes only with true repentance, brokenness and humility to enter in the Holy of Holies. A true worshipper goes beyond the veil and stay there long enough to get their release.

> ***"Send one of the exiled priests back to Samaria. Let him live there and teach the new residents the religious customs of the God of the land." 28 So one of the priests who had been exiled from Samaria returned to Bethel and taught the new residents how to worship the Lord"*** [2 King 17:25-28].

The anointing of greatness is an anointing of expanse [spread, or stretch]. It takes going beyond the veil and releasing your heart to God to receive and release heaven divine order into earthly situation. God is preparing you for greater. He desires to raise you up to teach others. God's timing is perfect. After you have come through your refining process, you will teach others how to endure and arise to say, ***"I Am Anointed For This."***

You are Being Redefined

Redefine means:-To define again or differently. It also means to re-examine or re-evaluate especially with a view to change. To be redefined is the process of transformation that brings forth power.

Are you a part of a group in the church or are you part of or among the 'REMNANT' in the church?

Too many people just exist as a part of the foundation of a church, but spend no quality time, cultivating, maintaining and building a personal relationship with God. Therefore, when trials and trouble comes, they react out of their flesh.

The Lord desires to raise up people who can be redefined and branded as *"I Am Anointed For This."* If you are just sitting in the pews for 35 years and complain about everything that should have or could have been different and refuse to reevaluate yourself this book is not for you!

Romans 12:1-2 says:-

> **"And so, dear brothers and sisters, I plead with you to give your bodies to God because of all he has done for you. Let them be a living and holy sacrifice—the kind he will find acceptable. This is truly the way to worship him. 2 Don't copy the behavior and customs of this world, but let God transform you into a new person by changing the way you think.**

Then you will learn to know God's will for you, which is good and pleasing and perfect."

Transformation has to do with a redefining moment that makes things change to something different. Redefining comes with transformation. Change takes hard work and discipline. Are you willing to suffer with Christ, in order to reign with Him? ***"I Am Anointed For This"*** means you are willing to bear the cross, endure the suffering to reign in the Glory of the Lord.

Philippians 3:10 ***"That I may know him, and the power of his resurrection, and the fellowship of his sufferings, being made conformable unto his death."***

To become TRANSFORMED [Redefined], as humans generally conveys that we are continuously making adjustments for others and our environments. However, in this season you are becoming redefined and transformed for the advancement of yourself into your ultimate purpose and destiny and as a result it positively influences you, others, and your environment.

When the refining process is over, you will see the implementation and manifestation of revolution in your character and condition that brands you as, ***"I Am Anointed For This."*** The Lord desires to raise up a remnant of people who have suffered some rejection, persecution, and ridicule. A remnant who has bared their cross, was buried in the tomb and suddenly rise up in the Glory.

They thought they were killing Jesus, but what they actually did was raise Him up three (3) days later into GLORY! As a result of which we are able to identify with the Messiah, *"The Anointed One."* To declare, ***"I Am Anointed For This"*** is God's ultimate plan and purpose to produce or bear fruit after His likeness as we take up our cross and follow Him. We want the "Lion of Judah" to come forth and take a stand, but we must surrender to His will first.

You must yield to God in this season like never before. The three Hebrew boys were presented with a death sentence. They had a choice of 'DO' or 'DIE'. You are ***'Anointed For This'*** not by default but your willingness to give up what is normal or comfortable. Average citizens of the kingdom are not ***"Anointed For This."*** The Hebrew boys were willing to sacrifice their lives for God! Their confidence in God was remarkable.

They made up their mind not to *"fall down and worship the golden image that Nebuchadnezzar hath set up"* [Daniel 3:5].

Shadrach, Meshach, and Abed-nego response was: - *"Nebuchadnezzar, we have no need to defend our actions in this matter. We are ready for the test. 17 If you throw us into the blazing furnace, then the God we serve is able to rescue us from a furnace of blazing fire and release us from your power, Your Majesty. 18 But even if He does not, O king, you can be sure that we still will not serve your gods and we will not worship the golden statue you erected"* [Daniel 3:16-18].

They could have rationalize the situation and pretend to be worshipping by bowing down and not actually worship the image or bow down just one time then ask for forgiveness. Instead, they choose not to violate God's command in Exodus 20:3, *"Do not worship other God's besides me."*

Even though all the excuses appears sensible, it is dangerous to rationalize. What excuse do you use for not standing up for God and endure the test?

Shadrach, Meshach and Abednego made up their minds not to lower the standard set by God, and to worship Him and Him alone. They were confident that God can and will deliver and,

> **"If you throw us in the fire, the God we serve can rescue us from your roaring furnace and anything else you might cook up, O king. But even if he doesn't, it wouldn't make a bit of difference, O king. We still wouldn't serve your gods or worship the gold statue you set up."**

Imagine the intensity of that heat turned up seven times hotter than it normally was heated. When the fiery trials increase in our lives many tend to regress. But we need to **"Dare to be bold"** like the Hebrew boys with confidence knowing that the God we serve is a promise keeper. A promise is a promise, that he will never leave us nor forsake us.
The refining process involves the goldsmith sitting right their over the fire, until all the dross is gone. He stays until he can sees his face shining through the gold.

Likewise in your refining process, the Holy Spirit sits there observing and watching over your refining process. He watches as the dross comes up: - Your mistakes, your shortcomings or doubts, our anxieties, your shame, your low-self-esteem, your longing to be accepted, your hurts and your pain and He loves you through it, patiently wait for the finish process, "PURE GOLD." Many will leave you for dead when you going through your "UGLY" season or process. Understand that, the "UGLY" represents the dross that surface first in the refining process. They will be quick to write you off as not fit for ministry or to be used by God. They my write you off as not being able to be a good mother, or make a good wife or husband!

But there is a God who loves you and watches your process to the end. When He is through with you the world will take notice. The anointing on your life will be in demand. You will begin to attract the right people into your life in this season. God will use the very thing you hate to try you in this season! It is not for naught because greater is coming that the world will take notice and God will get the glory. My advice to you, don't BOW!

Stay on the potter's wheel as He redefines your life and shape you for High and a Great Destiny.

Some people will attempt to throw you off your post and get you out of position with their criticism, persecution and mockery but the more they expose your flesh, God is saying you are just being crucified so you could be put into the tomb, so that *'I CAN RAISE YOU INTO THE GLORY!'* Declare it, **"I Am Being Raised Into Glory, I Am Anointed For This!"**

Some Biblical Strategies to Help You

- David quickly killed Goliath but waited patiently for God to deal with Saul.
- Although David was anointed to be Israel's next king, he had to wait years to realize this promise.
- The difficult circumstances in life and the times of waiting often refines, teach, and prepare us for the future responsibilities God has for us.
- Trials by fire, birth within you **"Fireproof Faith."** Proving that the strongest leaders are those who trust God to rule their lives.

- Your test is no accident. Remaining true to you faith, positions you to find favor with God and man.
- The trials by fire positions you to utilize your gifts and discover that, ***"I Am Anointed For This."***
- The trails by fire cause you to dig deep and uncover the resources and wealth of wisdom and knowledge stored up in you!
- You are being redefined and you are ***"Anointed For This."***

There are always consequences for not waiting on the Lord. This can be avoided if we keep at the forefront of our mind the promises of the Lord. The Hebrew boys kept the promises of God at the forefront of their minds that He is a protector and a deliverer. On the other hand, the Israelites wanted to help God out and demanded a King. They also had suffered from corrupt priest and judges as well. They insisted they wanted a king.

This represented conforming to the world system and the norms and tradition of the surrounding nations. Even though, it was against his original purpose, God chose a king for them [Saul] under whose hand they struggled. They had to endure and wait under that which they asked for, until God finally raised up a man after His own heart – DAVID. Israel's lack of patience and resistance to God's authority caused them to establish a monarch that did not solve problems.

God is removing every idol from your heart and your life. You cannot pour new wine into old wineskin. What God requires is the genuine devotion of each person's mind and heart to him. The Hebrew boys displayed that. David also displayed that. He knew how to wait before the Lord, as expressed throughout the Book of the Psalm. Psalm 34:10 says,

"The young lions do lack, and suffer hunger: but they that seek the Lord shall not want any good thing."

I implore you to wait before the Lord because when He is through with the refining process you will be redefined, you shall be as pure gold. Your redefining moment is NOW, don't bow. Declare it right now, **"I Am ANOINTED FOR THIS!"**

Chapter 7

I Am Coming Out Perfect

When all hell seems to be breaking through, east, west, north and south, so shall the blessings of the Lord over take you on every side.

The book of Job tells the story of Job, a faithful man of God. It is a gripping drama of riches-to-rags-to-riches, a theological discourse about suffering and the divine sovereignty of God as well as a vivid picture of faith that endures. As you read Job, evaluate your life and check your foundation. And may you be able to say that when all is gone but God, He is sufficient and ***"I Am Anointed For This."***

Job was a prosperous farmer living in the land of Uz. He had thousands of sheep, camels, and other livestock, a large family, and many servants. Suddenly, Satan the accuser came before God claiming that Job was trusting God only because he was wealthy and everything was going well for him. And so the testing of Job's faith began.

Job's First Test - Job 1:6-12

"One day the members of the heavenly court came to present themselves before the Lord, and the Accuser, Satan, came with them. 7 "Where have you come from?" the Lord asked Satan. Satan answered the Lord, "I have been patrolling the earth, watching everything that's going on." 8 Then the Lord asked Satan, "Have you noticed my servant Job? He is the finest man in all the earth. He is blameless—a man of complete integrity. He fears God and stays away from evil." 9 Satan replied to the Lord, "Yes, but Job has good reason to fear God. 10 You have always put a wall of protection around him and his home and his property. You have made him prosper in everything he does. Look how rich he is! 11 But reach out and take away everything he has, and he will surely curse you to your face!"*

12 "All right, you may test him," the Lord said to Satan. "Do whatever you want with everything he possesses, but don't harm him physically." So Satan left the Lord's presence."

Satan was allowed to destroy Job's children, servants, livestock, herdsmen, and home. Nevertheless, Job continued to trust in God.

'Have you been tested and have been tried, Satan the accuser has tried to destroy your life. Hurt, abuse, confused and used, but in spite of it all you still have joy.' You will find joy in the midst of your trial and circumstances because of your assurance, faith and hope in God's word. God is not a God to lie, nor the Son of Man to repent. Declare, **"I am Anointed For This"** and **"I Am Coming Out Perfect."**

I migrated to the United States of America to join my late husband Pastor Dr. Richard Manning in September 2003. The word was declared over my life by Pastor Anthony Francis as he released blessing and prayed over me that "*GOD IS TAKING YOU INTO GREATNESS*". Two months after entering the country, my husband had his first car accident in November 2003.

That was not the only one he had. He had over six accidents over the ten plus years living here as the enemy tried to do everything to frustrate "GREATNESS".

In March of 2004, doctors discovered a benign Myxoma in his left artery and was scheduled for surgery in June of that same year. That same month March 2004, we suffered the loss of our first six – eight week old fetus and was healing from the miscarriage. His surgery took place later that year. Call it a surgery gone badly. They opened his chest again in less than twelve (12) hours after the initial surgery. We fasted and we prayed and still this happened. But we never lost hope through this ordeal we kept focus on God and continue to worship and remain steadfast in the faith.

By October 2004 of the same year, I suffered another miscarriage. This time it was still birth after twenty two weeks in the pregnancy. For those who have been down this road, you can imagine how I felt. Having to hold the dead fetus in my arm as instructed by the nurse to get closure. I wept for days.

In the midst of all that each time I wept, it was like a well was springing up with a praise. The late, Pastor Dr. Richard Manning laid hands on me after four to five days and declared Isaiah 61, the oil of joy for mourning and the garment of praise for the spirit of heaviness.

For the remaining two to three weeks all I did was worship. In that moment, for the second time that year the Lord spoke to me again that, for your shame you shall possess the double. Pastor Dr. Richard Manning, was diagnosed with having had brain tumor and was divinely healed by God in 1996, a year before I entered bible college, where we met and shortly after got married.

His headaches were so severe, he had to lie on the benches when he attended church as a faithful Deacon, determined that God is a healer and the best place to be was in His presence. Every year since that after migrating to the United States, he did brain scans that prove that there was no trace of a tumor. I am saying this to say, that we know God is a healer. Over the course of our marriage he had several health challenges over the years but God will always come through.

Suddenly, 2006, we gave birth to triplets, all products of the divine miracle of prayer, prophetic intercession and worship as we endeavored to walk by faith. You test, furnace of afflictions prepares you for the "SUDDENLIES OF GOD." Who would have known that I would be able to carry triplet, but God!

Why am I sharing this? Satan buffets you, because one, his time is short. Two, it is just a test and you are ***"Coming Out Perfect."*** The doctors gave up on me, told me it was a slim chance of even carrying one baby to term. But God, impregnated my womb with multiples, without the help of fertility treatment. The doctors were even encouraging me to remove one of the fetus, because they see or consider me an at risk patient.

I told them, I didn't put them in there and if God wants to remove one, then He will do it His way, but killing one of the babies that God divinely placed in their was not going to happen. I know the birth of the triplets was a miracle, with multiple fibroids like grapefruit, it wasn't even supposed to be possible to carry one, less three. This is what you call a miracle, God's supernatural intervention, as my late husband and I choose to worship, pray and remain faithful to the Lord and His processing.

Job 1:18-21

"While he was still speaking, another messenger arrived with this news: "Your sons and daughters were feasting in their oldest brother's home. 19 Suddenly, a powerful wind swept in from the wilderness and hit the house on all sides. The house collapsed, and all your children are dead. I am the only one who escaped to tell you."
20 Job stood up and tore his robe in grief. Then he shaved his head and fell to the ground to worship.
21 He said, "I came naked from my mother's womb, and I will be naked when I leave. The Lord gave me what I had, and the Lord has taken it away. Praise the name of the Lord!"

The Lord took my husband home to glory on May 31, 2014 after a severe two year (2) battle with his health. The devil doesn't win even in the death of the saints. We have the victory even in death. The enemy could not touch him without God's permission. Pastor Dr. Richard Manning finished his course, fulfilled His ultimate purpose in the last three (3) years of His life. He was definitely ***"Anointed For This!"*** Jesus ministry on earth was also three (3) years, after which He transition into the Glory to be with the God the Father.

Our ministry and our lives was always surrounded and cultivated with prayer and worship constantly and intensified over the last three years up to His death since the ministry started. In fact we met at an all-day prayer meeting at Bible College. Our marriage foundation was built on prayer and the Word of God, and still I maintain that fervency in my life and the ministry.

When I replay some of our preaching videos on You Tube, I reflect on three and a half years ago we stepped out by faith to respond to God's call on our lives. My late husband Dr. Pastor-Richard Manning was very quiet by nature, but was a prolific, profound teacher of the word with a prophetic flow. Even though, he never wanted to be in the forefront, he would rather do one and one evangelism, he created a dynamic impact on all those who hear his messages, and received encouragement or counsel through him from the Lord.

Dr. Myles Munroe just died this week as I am getting ready to publish this book, is such a confirmation that God anoints us on purpose and chose us for His glory. Dr. Myles Munroe was one his favorite speakers and he also invested in his books. One of Dr. Munroe's quote are, **"You are not important because of how long you live, you are important because of how effective you live,"**

Pastor Dr. Richard was chosen for a unique purpose, he was **'Anointed For This'** and he lived out his purpose and effected change through his words and lifestyle. Are you living out your purpose effectively? Are you *'Anointed for This'* and living on purpose. God has designed you for the assignment given to you. The things you have to go through for the anointing is what he uses to design you for purpose and destiny.

What if we never answered the call three years ago?

He would have died and not fulfill his ultimate purpose. When God calls you expect opposition but it is better to please God than man. If I had listened to what man said I would have regrets now! But I praise God for the "SHIFT" and I am thankful that Pastor Dr. Richard Manning fulfilled his purpose.

He birthed out through Prophetic in Warfare Deliverance and Worship Tabernacle what we discuss on our honeymoon his desire to help the community. "Men with a Mission" Evangelism Outreach for visiting the sick or elderly, prison ministry, the food pantry and shelter outreach to the community with a global thrust were birthed out in November 2012.

If you are in a dry place and it seems like it won't be over, in the church "IT IS TIME TO SHIFT". Many are loyal religiously to a church and sit in the pews dying, waiting to go to heaven. What have you done with your talents and gifts? Get in a place where God can use them.

My husband would go to the church every morning to pray in the sanctuary and still come home to have quiet time with the Lord and study the word of God. During this battle with his health over the last two years to his transition into Glory I say the miracles of God still in operation. He was bed ridden, could hardly get to the bathroom by himself. Someone say, but God, on December 31st, the Holy Spirit as a ball of fire, entered our bedroom in the form of a global shape ball of fire and rested upon him as I interceded and worshipped in the Spirit. That day, God raised him up off his sick bed. I was praying for months asking God for a notable miracle.

That same evening, he cut all three boys hair. Pastor Dr. Richard Manning was unable to cut their hair for the past eight months to that time. The boys were so delighted they woke me from my nap to let me know. For the remaining five months of his life after that, he never missed church except on Mother's Day. On May 12, 2014, the day after Mother's day, he was hospitalized. Even when he was in the hospital on previous occasions, he would dial into the church services using the church by phone prayer line.

When he was in church he worshipped. His favorite posture was to bow down and worshipped God as the glory descends.

It took him a while to dress but he was determine to enter the gates of the Lord with thanksgiving and into the courts of God with praise. These challenges with his health, especially the last year to his death happened as I care for my children, and function as the Apostle of the ministry.

His health challenges was meant for me to throw in the towel, but God strengthened me because "I Choose To Worship" the Lord and remain constant in my faith. When the enemy touch everything you have, and try to take your mind or discourage you in the interim, do like Job, bow down and worship, because it is not over until God says it is over. Hallelujah, Lord, I thank you.

> *Job stood up and tore his robe in grief. Then he shaved his head and fell to the ground to worship. 21 He said, "I came naked from my mother's womb, and I will be naked when I leave. The Lord gave me what I had, and the Lord has taken it away. Praise the name of the Lord!" 22 In all of this, Job did not sin by blaming God"*
> [Job 1:20-22].

Next Satan attacked Job physically, covering him with painful sores. Job's wife told him to curse God and die (Job 2:9), but Job suffered in silence. I felt like this for a moment, I suffered in silence. Those we looked up to and revered in ministry who knew he was ill and kept them informed, turned a blind eye to what we were going through, didn't even visit him while he was sick, not even once. Nonetheless, we still choose to worship God and walk in forgiveness.

Three of Job's friends, Eliphaz, Bildad, and Zophar, came to visit him. At first they silently grieved with Job. But when they began to talk about the reasons for Job's tragedies, they told him that sin had caused his suffering. They told him to confess his sins and turn back to God. But Job maintained his innocence.

We maintained our innocence, as speculations, accusations, mockery and judgments were hurled at us. Job's friends were unable to convince Job of his sin, the three men fell silent (Job 32:1). At this point, another voice, the young Elihu, entered the debate. Although his argument also failed to convince Job, it prepared the way for God to speak.

Can I tell you something, your trial by fire, is preparing God to speak on your behalf. It has placed a demand on heaven for supernatural release and intervention. The people who left you for dead, thought you never would have made it, prepares you for divine intervention from God. It places you under pressure when you back is against the wall. Trials and tribulation one after another forces you to keep your eyes on the Lord and places a demand on Heaven.

This journey has prepared God to speak into my life in this season. This journey has also allowed Pastor Dr. Richard Manning's life and ministry to be a great legacy, memorial and testimony to advance the kingdom of God. Pastor Dr. Richard Manning lived out his purpose: - ***"The greatest tragedy in life is not death, but a life without a purpose"*** [Dr. Myles Munroe].

Many times we pray for God to deliver loved ones from battles they face, often times it is done here on earth. Other times God delivered them by giving them a new body, taking them home to be with him in heaven. The greatest and ultimate healing is the assurance that they died in the Lord.

"When you die, it does not mean that you lose to sickness," "You beat sickness by how you live, why you live, and in the manner in which you live. R.I.P. Pastor Dr. Richard Manning, [February 15, 1969 – May 31st, 2014].

"You "LIVED" for Christ and "DIED" in Christ a full life!!! You will always be remembered for your standard for righteousness, holiness, a man who was on a mission for God!!! Your children remember how you prayed with them each morning, and taught them the word of God. Now, your legacy lives on!!!"

You can rest in the Lord and His promises because He has a ***'Master Plan'*** for our lives and nothing that you go through will be wasted. Fasten your seat belt [Gird up your loins with truth], **"THE GLORY IS JUST AROUND THE CORNER."** Rejoice, that you are **"Coming out Perfect."** God is getting ready to give you double for your shame and your pain you have endured. Your latter will be greater than your past.

Chapter 8

The Glory Is Just Around The Corner

"Friends, when life gets really difficult, don't jump to the conclusion that God isn't on the job. Instead, be glad that you are in the very thick of what Christ experienced. This is a spiritual refining process, with glory just around the corner" [1 Peter 4:12-16, The Message].

I can write with confidence., ***"I Am Anointed For This!"*** because God strengthened me in ways I cannot express in words during our marriage of fourteen (14) years as we went through trials and battles with his health and also, during the period we lost two babies by miscarriage. Out of that came double for our trouble, according to Isaiah 61:7:-

"Instead of your shame [ye shall have] double; instead of confusion they shall celebrate with joy their portion:

> **therefore in their land they shall possess the double; everlasting joy shall be unto them.**

Our marriage produced four (4) children conceived within two (2) pregnancies for the loss of two (2) miscarriages. Do the math, two times two equals four [2 x 2 = 4].

I want tell you that for every season of test and trials you endure there is a new level of glory that shall arise upon your life. There is a new level of blessing that shall be released to you. The anointing is not made on the mountain top, it is made through the valley experiences, the trials by fire [In the valley]. David was left on the back side to tend to the sheep's, there he had many challenges, fighting bears and lions to protect the sheep. He experienced rejection from his family, but still he never took his focus off God nor his post in God. He maintained his faith and stance in the Lord.

David maintained communion and fellowship with the Lord through prayer, worship and meditation on God's promises. When trials come, learn from David's experiences, and hold fast to the promises of

God that has been given to you. Keep them at the forefront of your mind and spirit.

Meditate on God's promises day and night according to Joshua 1:8, because this brings forth success and supernatural provision and prosperity.

When the time came for selection for the 'Kingly Anointing', he was forgotten as a son. When Samuel came to Jessie's house to anoint the pre-destined King, Jessie called each son except for David. But Samuel said, **"Is there yet not another!"**

God has not forgotten you, even when man forgets God keeps records. Jessie called all his other sons to get in line but Samuel did not discern any of these. It doesn't matter who or what situations in your life pushed you to the back or make you feel like you are of no value or unusable, God's glory is around the corner just for you. Doctors gave us no hope after the miscarriages, but God says, not so.
Your faith rises in the storm as you maintain your confidence and trust in the Lord, like David.

Your faith shifts you in position, regardless of who crowds you out or circumstances that has given you a push back for over 10 years, for some 12 years or it seems like one after another the trials come crashing in. The level of your warfare, is an indicator of the weight of glory you will carry and the level of abundance God has for you. No experience in your life will be wasted.

God blessed us with four (4) children, eight years old triplet – two boys and a girl, Abigail, Aaron and Nathaniel. We naturally conceived them without any fertility treatment and later on we had a six (6) year old boy who broke through all methods used to prevent pregnancies to fulfill what "double" means; Two miscarriage times two pregnancies is four, do the math, [2 x 2 = 4]. Shout Glory!

On the evening Pastor Dr. Richard Manning died, May 31, 2014, the Lord told me to have a 90 minutes Prophetic Celebration of his life the next day as our Sunday Worship Experience. For his home going service, it was themed, ***"Prophetic Celebration of the Life of Pastor Dr. Richard Manning."*** Powerful testimonies came forth from family and friends who we have not seen for years or even met before about the refreshing they experience at the service. One of his cousins from New York gave her life to, Christ, led by a minister friend of mine who sat next to her and also kept contact with her after Pastor Dr. Richard Manning Homecoming Service.

Moreover, another cousin joined our ministry from New York, because of the Prophetic Encounter she experienced at the Homecoming Service of Pastor Dr. Richard Manning. Testimonies are still coming forth. Talk about God's goodness, and using the things that was meant to kill you to show forth His praise and glory. Five (5) days after Pastor Dr. Richard Manning Homecoming and Prophetic Celebration of life, I had to journey to North Carolina to preach at a revival.

This was already set in motion from February 2014, confirmed and my airline ticket was sent via email by the Apostle of that church. By April the Lord gave me the word for that house, ***"RIDE OUT THE STORM"***! God knew He would take Richard home and my journey have been and was just that, "RIDE OUT THE STORM"! I knew I had to obey God regardless of what was happening to me and the loss of my husband. It is far better to obey God first, and then discover the reasons later. We are never free to disobey God just because we don't understand.

In the revival in North Carolina, generational curses were broken, lives healed, restored, financial breakthrough, and revival. Pentecostal revival took place. My testimony and experience with my husband health challenge and his death became a pivotal shifting for lives to be transformed. I understand clearly what the Bible reveals that even in death there is victory and God is glorified.

I can encourage you through this book to ride out your storm. ***"RIDE OUT YOUR STORM"*** my sister, my brothers, you are coming out perfect and God will get the glory out of it. Say, ***"I AM ANOINTED FOR THIS*****!"** By August 2014, two (2) months later, I went to Jamaica to handle some business because of his death, in the interim hosted a two day conference called, **"MEGA-MIND ~ MEGA-KINGDOM Prophetic Circuit"**.

It was a supernatural release and outpouring of the Lord's presence like fresh wind and fire blowing in the midst. A prophetic flow like none other as lives were transformed, healing, miracles and breakthrough took place at a greater level. This opened even more doors for approximately another week of ministering.

I was able to use my experience and testimony of ministering to my husband during his health challenge and even in his death, to speak life, healing and restoration to others.

One Bishop, said, this anointing on your life is unique and it is hard to find a women in Jamaica with that level of anointing on their lives to do ministry to bring forth deliverance to the people, especially identifying with what women are going through right now.

Listen, when things seem overwhelming, challenging, life threatening to the point of feeling like you are about to lose your mind, God's getting ready to move unprecedentedly in your life, marriage, family and or ministry. When something happens in your life in the form of a setback, even painful as the loss of a loved one, you have to decide to either go forward or sit there and grieve continually.

Trust the God with the "Master Plan", who has already foreknew and predestinated that you are ***"Anointed For This"*** and forge ahead into your season of greater grace, favor, expansion and blessings.

***"For I know the plans I have for you,"
says the Lord. "They are plans for good
and not for disaster, to give you a
future and a hope"*** [Jeremiah 29:11].

Testimony of Smith Wigglesworth

Dr. Robert Lairdon did years of research on all the legendary men and women who have blazed the trail of Pentecostal Revivals across the globe for Jesus Christ. He shared on the life of Smith Wigglesworth in a documentary that when Wigglesworth wife died, Wigglesworth grieved for a while, then decided to move forward.

What happened next was that, Smith Wigglesworth ministry expanded to a greater dimension as he began travelling to South Africa, New Zealand, Australia and to America many times. Wigglesworth got up and made the pain a positive step.

When you are going through something that is challenging or have experienced the loss of a loved one or spouse grieve for that moment, then get up – "Rise Up." Go do something bigger, louder, larger and better.

"Make the devil pay for it and make your life count in the Kingdom as Smith Wigglesworth did" [Robert Lairdon]. Dr. Robert Lairdon, further quoted what his grandmother always said: - ***"DON'T DIE UNTIL YOU ARE DEAD!"*** Do something for God and do it LOUD and do it BOLD!

Declare it today, ***"I AM ANOINTED FOR THIS"*** *and God is preparing me for greater.* ***"The Greater Glory Is Just Around The Corner."***

Greater Comes With a Price

I hear the Spirit of the Lord saying: -

> ***These things saith He that is holy, He that is true, He that hath the key of David, He that openeth, and no man shutteth; and shutteth and no man openeth; I know thy works: behold, I have set before thee an open door, and no man can shut it: for thou hast a little strength, and hast kept My word, and hast not denied My name.***

In the latter chapters of the book of Job, God

finally spoke out of a mighty storm. Confronted with the great power and majesty of God, Job fell in humble reverence before God—speechless. God rebuked Job's friends, and the drama ended with Job restored to happiness and wealth. Can I tell you, the drama has come to an end in your life, in your children(s) life, in your ministry and in your home?

When all hell seems to be breaking loose to the east, west, north and south, so shall the blessings of the Lord over take you on every side. God is getting ready to blow your mind with blessings and unprecedented favor.

He has set before you open doors that no man can shut. Even though, it seem like you have little strength right now, that's when Jesus step out to blow your mind with His promises and to let you know that delay is not denial. Wake up look for God's blessings every day. Expect it, unprecedented favor, divine healing, restoration and blessings. I believe and receive it for myself. Like Job you will say,

"I had only heard about you before, but now I have seen you with my own eyes.

6 I take back everything I said, and I sit in dust and ashes to show my repentance" [Job 42:5].

"I Am Anointed For This" means you have paid the price, you have experienced the Lord of the valley and the mountain, and not just hearing it from someone else. You have experience the Lord who giveth and taketh and also who can make all things new. Like Job, you have encountered the God who is now taking you into a **"New Beginning."** I hear the Spirit of the Lord saying, ***"Forget the former things for behold I am doing a new thing.***" It is a New Season, embrace the next Dimension because GREATER IS COMING!

Job said: - ***"I had heard rumors about you, but now my eyes have seen you"*** [Job 42:5]

When God says he is taking you into greatness, expect opposition, persecution, trials and attacks to come, but let nothing separate you from the love of God which is in Christ Jesus our Lord. God will raise you up to bring deliverance to the same ones who left you for dead, who talked about you and misunderstood you and what you were going through.

What was the conclusion of the whole matter?
<u>The Lord Blesses Job</u> - Job 42:7-11

"After the Lord had finished speaking to Job, he said to Eliphaz the Temanite: "I am angry with you and your two friends, for you have not spoken accurately about me, as my servant Job has. 8 So take seven bulls and seven rams and go to my servant Job and offer a burnt offering for yourselves. My servant Job will pray for you, and I will accept his prayer on your behalf. I will not treat you as you deserve, for you have not spoken accurately about me, as my servant Job has." 9 So Eliphaz the Temanite, Bildad the Shuhite, and Zophar the Naamathite did as the Lord commanded them, and the Lord accepted Job's prayer. 10 When Job prayed for his friends, the Lord restored his fortunes. In fact, the Lord gave him twice as much as before! 11 Then all his brothers, sisters, and former friends came and feasted with him in his home. And they consoled

him and comforted him because of all the trials the Lord had brought against him. And each of them brought him a gift of money and a gold ring.

Greater comes with a price. It comes with the shaking, the crushing, the beating and the pressing for the oil to run. You are coming out perfect and you will truly and boldly declare ***"I AM ANOINTED FOR THIS!"*** Moreover, what didn't kill you is getting ready to promote you.

Your latter end [season] will be greater than the former. It is a 'NEW SEASON' coming to you that will make you known and for sure testify Romans 8:28 that says, ***"And we know that all things work together for good to them that love God, to them who are the called according to his purpose."***

For your shame you shall receive the double portion. This is your season of grace and favor to reap what you have sewn.

"So the Lord blessed Job in the second half of his life even more than in the beginning. For now he had 14,000 sheep, 6,000 camels, 1,000 teams of oxen, and 1,000 female donkeys. 13 He also gave Job seven more sons and

three more daughters. 14 He named his first daughter Jemimah, the second Keziah, and the third Keren-happuch. 15 In all the land no women were as lovely as the daughters of Job. And their father put them into his will along with their brothers. 16 Job lived 140 years after that, living to see four generations of his children and grandchildren" [Job 42:12-16].

You were anointed for this, and the stirring of God is shifting you into a greater place. You were already anointed to pass the test. God allowed you to go through that test because He trust you and knew you would pass the test. Romans 8:29 declares,

"For whom he did foreknow, he also did predestinate to be conformed to the image of his Son, that he might be the firstborn among many brethren."

God knew you before you were born and the anointing on your life and the greatness in store for you was already pre-determined or predestinated. The Lord knew you would have to suffer some on the journey into greatness. Greatness is birthed out of the tests, trials and persecution you experience. When you endure to the end, there will be a greater increase in your life of God's miracles and supernatural intervention and abundance.

This includes new and greater divine connection, destiny help, uncommon provision, blessings and open doors that no man can shut. **YOUR ARE COMING OUT PERFECT!** My challenge to you right now at the close of this chapter is, ***"What kind of praise will you give God for the promises resting over your heads?"*** I double dare you to demonstrate that kind of praise in advance RIGHT NOW!!! It's praise break time!

I decree and declare that there is a window over your head with 'Blessings! Blessings! Blessings! What Kind of praise are you getting ready to release out of your belly "NOW?" Shout Hallelujah, and declare ***"I Am Anointed for This"*** – ***So go ahead and give Him all the praise!***

Prophetic Declaration Prayer

I declare and declare that I will live a long and full life, fulfilling my purpose and destiny in the name of Jesus. I thank you Lord that my latter is and will be greater than my past. As the scripture says, Job second half was greater than his beginning. I am coming out perfect into a greater place in God, double for my trouble.

I thank you Lord now for my double portion, men shall give into my bosom double blessings, the anointing of kindness and unprecedented favor is upon me, and men are hastening to help me, support and bless me. I decree and declare blessings unsurmountable and unstoppable are released to me now in Jesus name, AMEN!

Chapter 9

Your Anointing and Blessing Has Been Predestinated

The anointing that you were designed to carry, has not only been tailor made for you, but it was already pre-determined by the Lord.

"Blessed be the God and Father of our Lord Jesus Christ, who hath blessed us with all spiritual blessings in heavenly places in Christ: 4 according as he hath chosen us in him before the foundation of the world, that we should be holy and without blame before him in love: 5 having predestinated us unto the adoption of children by Jesus Christ to himself, according to the good pleasure of his will, 6 to the praise of the glory of his grace, wherein he hath made us accepted in the beloved" [Ephesians 1:3-6]

Being predestinated by God means that it has been prearranged, and destined for us to be His sons and daughters to inherit all spiritual blessings in heavenly places [Ephesians 1]. Predestined also means appointed, preordained or foreordained. Your anointing, blessings and destiny was foreordained by a divine decree or purpose. God has decided long before we were formed in our mother's womb our divine and eternal destiny. You cannot know the will of the Lord for your life without the mind of Christ. The mind denotes generally the seat of reflective consciousness, comprising the faculties' of perception and understanding those feelings. The minds judges and determines in any given situation.

1 Corinthians 2:16 declares that, ***"For who hath known the mind of the Lord, that he may instruct him? But we have the mind of Christ"***.

Through our union with Christ, we have access to Christ's mind, Christ's divine thoughts, and Christ's counsel.

Let this mind be in you, which was also in Christ Jesus [Philippians 2:5]. To have the mind of Christ and let His mind be in us, we must submit ourselves to God. Our obedience in serving comes from abiding in the word of God [St. John 15:1-8]. The mind becomes transformed as it is renewed day by day in the Word of the Lord. It requires denying yourself, taking up the cross and follow Christ.

You are already blessed. Your blessings has been pre-determined by God, all He wants you to do is come out of the mentality of Egypt and worship Him in Spirit and in truth. The Israelites were in bondage in Egypt and God heard their cry and sent a deliverer. The blessings that God has for you was already predestined and established through Abraham to rest upon us that have been engrafted into the family tree of God (Gentiles through the shed blood of Jesus Christ).

Galatians 3:14 *"**This is what God had in mind all along: the blessing He gave to Abraham might extend to all nations through the Anointed One, Jesus; and we are the beneficiaries of this promise**"*

of the Spirit that comes only through faith."

To walk into the things God has for you, your mind must be transformed to think upon Jesus as the rock of the church. He call us to a perpetual relationship and covenant with Him as Hebrew 8:10 explains:-

"For this is the covenant that will make the house of Israel after those days, says the Lord: I will put my laws in their mind and write them on their hearts; and I will be their God, and they shall be My people."

When our hearts are transformed, it will not be difficult to yield and follow the path into your purpose, destiny and the blessings that God has for us. As we submit to the Lord, He gives us the innate desire to follow His directions. As a result of this the Kingdom automatically becomes our life style. Ephesians 1:11-14 reveals that, long before the foundations were laid, he had us on His mind to establish us into His promises.

What God has for us was divinely chosen and predestinated through the sacrificial death of Jesus Christ. It is only through His sacrifice that this privilege is given to us, being adopted as joint heirs to the throne of grace. It was God's unchanging plan from the beginning that we walk in the fullness of the God-Head.

God chose you and when He looks at you, He sees you through His Spiritual eyes. The level of your anointing is also a precursor for the blessing to flow. Knowing that our blessings were already predestinated, gives us the reassurance to trust God at His word. Why? Joshua 23:3b reminds us that, ***"because it is the Lord your God who was fighting for you"***. God was and is fighting for you to enter into everything He has for you.

Joshua is six years old and I told him November 03, 2014 at bedtime to select a scripture so we can do for his devotion and this was the scripture he chose. Then he went on to explain that, *"God is winning for you. God is protecting you from danger and from anyone who will try to kidnap you."* It had me searching the whole chapter and meditating on the revelation that flowed from this chapter into chapter 24.

"I decree and declare that, the plans of the enemy to highjack or [kidnap] your destiny in this season is destroyed in the name of Jesus. Satan is defeated and God is exalted in the name of Jesus."

In this season of your life and or ministry, marriage, family or business or business plans God has positioned you in a place *"Without Walls and Without Limits!"* You have been through some hardship and struggles and what felt like bondage [Egypt], but that which or what hindered you, I hear the Lord says *"My Spirit has lifted a standard."* He has ***"plagued [your] Egypt, according to what I did among them; Afterward I brought you out"*** [Joshua 24:5]. Verse 7 says, ***"So they cried out to the Lord, and He put darkness between you and the Egyptians, brought the sea upon them, and covered them"***.

God says, *"I have covered every trap of the enemy with darkness, they will not be able to discover, find, hinder or block you anymore"*.

For a season you were in the wilderness, but I have placed darkness between you and your enemies that they cannot touch you or block you. Moreover, just as I caused the Red Sea to cover Pharaoh, his horsemen and chariots, so I will allow you to enter in and possess your enemies land. God will give it to you in this season, ***"The land of the Amorites, who dwelt on the other side of Jordan..."***

Say this as a Prophetic Declaration that: -

>*"What God did for Israel He is doing right now in my life, I have and will continue to possess the gates of my enemies, and I will succeed. Everything that I touch shall be blessed, where I walk I shall be blessed and all shall be blessed in Jesus name,* ***"I AM ANOINTED FOR THIS."***

According to Joshua Chapter 24, God would not let Balaam, speak anything else but blessing on Israel, even though he tried to carry out Balak wishes God blocked it. Say out loud: - **GOD BLOCKED IT! Oh Yes HE did!!!** Even right now in Jesus name. God has given over your enemies into your hand that you might possess their land and He has destroyed them before you. Even if they try to pray or speak a curse over you, God will not permit them.

Joshua 24:9-11 **" When Balak, son of Zippor, king of Moab, decided to attack Israel, he called on Balaam, the son of Beor, to curse you, 10 but I would not listen to Balaam. All he could do was bless you. I delivered you out of his clutches. 11 When you crossed over the Jordan into the land of Canaan and came to Jericho, the leaders[a] of Jericho fought against you. So did the Amorites, the Perizzites, the Canaanites, the Hittites, and the Jebusites. But I gave them all into your power."**

What God has for you is for you. He is about to give you lands, blessings and financial outpouring you did not even work for.

Joshua 24:12-14 **"I sent hornets ahead of you to run off the two kings of the Amorites; it was not done by your bow or sword. 13 I delivered to you fields you had not worked and towns you had not built, yet today you live in them.**

> ***You eat the fruit of olive trees and of grape vineyards you did not even have to plant." 14 So remember: fear the Eternal and serve Him sincerely and faithfully. Put away from you any gods your ancestors served across the Euphrates River or in Egypt, and serve only Him."***

All He ask for you to do is to serve Him, and to worship Him in Spirit and in truth. Chapter 7 of my first book *"Awake to Your Destiny" Volume 1, "The Mind of Christ"* explains that, God is in the business of restoration, renewal, re-birth and revival and you will reap if you faint not. You have been chosen by God to bear fruit, and the fruit shall remain. Forsake your will, and yield yourself to God's will. As you submit to His will your process of being shaped into a clearer picture of Christ [His Image and likeness] gradually conforms you to the image of your predestinated purpose and position.

Awake to your destiny and believe God, that He has chosen you and you have a place in history. Yes, He has chosen you, you have a place in history and you are right for the part. Declare it today and speak it out loud: - **"I AM ANOINTED FOR THIS** and **MY ANOINTING AND MY BLESSING HAS BEEN PREDESTINATED BY GOD.**

Prophetic Declaration

I decree and declare and command the blessings of the Lord upon my life. I dare to believe what God's promises say over my life! I decree and declare that today!

Today my DESTINY IS COMING INTO IT'S FULNESS! My BREAKTHROUGH IS COMING INTO FRUITION! I Am At My TURNING POINT! In Jesus Mighty Name! I speak BREAKTHROUGH, in the name of Jesus! It's a New Day, It's A New Season, and IT'S A NEW BLESSINGS!!! Hallelujah!!!

I decree the rain of His presence has come upon my life, the rain to enrich me, the rain to prosper me, the rain to restore me, the rain to refresh me, the rain to catapult me in the name of Jesus! Amen! "I AM ANOINTED FOR THIS."

Apostle Dr. Nadine Manning Biography

Apostle Dr. Nadine Manning was born and raised in Spanish Town, Jamaica. She was happily married for fourteen years to the late, Pastor, Dr. Richard Manning who transitioned into Glory to be with the Lord on May 31st 2014. Together they had eight (8) year old triplet Abigail, Aaron, and Nathaniel and six (6) years old Joshua Manning; all products of the miracles of prayer and prophetic intercession.

Apostle, Dr. Nadine Manning, migrated to the U.S.A. in September 2003 and presently has her ministry base in Millville, New Jersey. Apostle Dr. Nadine and the late, Pastor, Dr. Richard Manning are the founder of Prophetic in Warfare Deliverance and Worship Tabernacle, New GAPIW Kingdom Fellowship and Genius Kids Academy & Learning Institute all are fully and duly Incorporated and located in Millville, NJ USA.

Apostle Dr. Nadine Manning holds Degrees in Theology, Business Administration and Public Administration. On May 18, 2014, she received her Doctorate in Theology from City of Hope Bible College.

Apostle, Dr. Nadine Manning

- Apostle Dr. Nadine roots in ministry developed and emerged through the Open Bible Standard of Churches, in Jamaica. Everyone affectionately called her A.K.A. Prophetess during her ministry in Jamaica.

- This organized body has its home-based affiliation to the Open Bible Standard Churches in the U.S.A. She started out as a Choir Member, Praise and Worship Leader, Sunday School Teacher, Drama Production minister as well as always busy doing street evangelism.

- She's known to always have a listening ear to counsel the youths her peers and also married women. Even while she was single they looked to her for the wise counsel that flowed through her as a young minister of the gospel of Jesus Christ.

- Prior to migrating to the U.S.A. she launched a Sunday School Outreach at her home to teach and empower the children and their parents after church in the evening.

- Apostle, Dr. Nadine Manning had a burning passion to minister to the loss on a buses, taxi-cabs, flea markets and the by-ways while living in Jamaica. She enjoys doing tent revivals/crusades.

- She visited New York three times since her stay in America and the unction of the Spirit came upon her where she was provoked to proclaim the word of God in the train cabins, prophetically.

- Apostle, Dr. Nadine Manning has been ministering and operating in the office of a
- Prophet, Prophetic Renegade Worshipping Warrior and Evangelical Preacher and teacher for over 15 years.
- She was ordained in Jamaica in the year 2000 as a License Minister of the gospel to function in her God given gifts and talents by the Lord under the Open Bible Standard Churches.
- Apostle, Dr. Nadine Manning has always been affectionately called *'Prophetess'* by her peers, leaders and renown in her field of ministry as Prophetess.
- In 2003 she migrated to the U.S.A. where she was again licensed by Rev. Willie Johnson Sr. as an Evangelist in the Eureka Baptist Church, in Wildwood. There she served for three (3) before relocating to Millville New Jersey. There she was accepted with license to serve as minister at Greater Deliverance Church in Vineland NJ under the leadership of Pastor Nathaniel Floyd until the Lord commissioned them in 2011 to launch Prophetic in Warfare Deliverance and Worship Tabernacle.
- This ministry, which initially began as a teaching ministry in Jamaica through Apostle, Dr. Nadine Manning.
- She taught on Prophetic in Warfare at a theological college in Jamaica and also assisted Pastor Anthony Francis in training the intercessors for two (2) years at Bethel Open Bible Church.

- She ministered across Jamaica doing revivals and conferences with Remnant Ministries International.
- Apostle, Dr. Nadine has a passion for intercession and sang with Pastor Richard Manning on several occasions at our services.
- They hosted a series of Prophetic Watch of the Lord services, teachings on the Ministry of the Watchman and Prophetic Intercession, The Priesthood of the Believer and more. The vision continues...
- She has a Global Mandate to teach, train and release intercessors, worshippers and all Kingdom Ambassadors into their position as a Watchman.
- The Apostolic anointing on her life enables her to identify gifts in the life of others and speak a life changing word to catapult them into their purpose and release them into the next dimension.
- She has a great passion for intercession and standing in the gap for others and the nations to see lives change, souls saved and transformation globally.
- Apostle, Dr. Nadine Manning is a global teacher, preacher, prophetic psalmist, and prolific writer that functions in the fivefold anointing.
- She is God's Apostolic Midwife who carries a dynamic anointing and Apostolic Revelatory Wisdom and Knowledge of the Word of God and God's End Time Movement and Revelation to the Body of Christ. She is the Apostolic Voice to the Nations.

History of Pastoral Ministry

- Apostle, Dr. Nadine Manning and the late Pastor, Dr. Richard Manning both has approximately 20 to 25 years in ministry overall.
- Almost three (3) years ago, Apostle, Dr. Nadine and the late, Pastor, Dr. Richard Manning had a desire to establish a church to show the love of God and to help the people in the community.
- Apostle, Dr. Nadine continues with fervency the vision and passion for winning souls for the body of Christ so that people will be healed and restored to their rightful place in God and to walk in their purpose.
- Together they established **Prophetic in Warfare Deliverance and Worship Tabernacle** in March 2011 and officially opened the doors for church in June 2011 in Millville, New Jersey. **New Birth Global Apostolic Prophetic in Warfare Kingdom Fellowship Inc.** is the governing body and organization for:

    o Prophetic in Warfare Deliverance and Worship Tabernacle a 501(c) (3),
    o Deborah's Daughter Company Inc.,
    o Apostle Nadine Manning Ministries Inc., [Woman of Worth, Jamaica],
    o Genius Kids Academy and Learning Institute Inc. and

- o Prophetic in Warfare Institute [School of the Prophets and Biblical Studies].
- This is a nondenominational global ministry established for **'Kingdom Purpose and Assignment'** where signs and wonders and miracles are in the midst.
- Prophetic in Warfare Deliverance and Worship Tabernacle began in Jamaica as a teaching ministry.
- The vision and passion through the ministry is to help the people in the community who are hopeless, defeated, victims of abuse, and living in poverty.

The following accomplishments testify to their character and integrity in ministry and confirms that which was already said in this biography:-

The Vision

The vision they co-founded together, Prophetic in Warfare Deliverance and Worship Tabernacle is to enable people to be empowered and completely released to walk into their God-given purpose and assignment through the teaching and demonstration of God's Word and the unction of Holy Spirit, to advance the Kingdom of God in the earth preaching deliverance and setting the captives free, (Isaiah 61:1-6). Their passion in birthing this ministry is to increase the people's knowledge as it relates to the word of God with a strong emphasis on Prophetic Intercession, Spiritual Warfare, Deliverance and Worship.

Achievements/Awards – Apostle Nadine and the Late Pastor Richard Manning

- **In January 2013**, Apostle Nadine and the late Pastor Richard Manning were recognized and received the Martin Luther King Award of Excellence by the Cumberland County Clerk. And the City of Vineland Mayor as 2013 Martin Luther King Jr Honorees for their hard work and dedication in the Cumberland County Community.

    o This is an outstanding achievement given their short term as Pastors in this region, even though they have over 20 years in ministry, this was a new territory for them, and have experienced a lot of spiritual warfare and challenges.

- Inspite of this they have accomplished a lot compare to other ministries that existed for many years, and the fact that they were not well known nor were they familiar people in the area.
- **In May 2014, Apostle, Dr. Nadine and Pastor, Dr. Richard received their Doctorate in Theology as well as Pastors of Excellence Award 2014 from City of Hope Bible College.**
- **February 2013** ~ The ministry launched the Kingdom Graphics Designo Inc. offering epic and outside of the box:- Banners, Brochures, T-Shirts, Funeral, Birthdays, Church Services programs, and Ministry Advertisement, Flyers and Movie Trailers and Graphic Designs

- **April 2013** ~ Apostle Nadine Manning became an Author in 2013, publishing her 1st book **"Awake to Your Destiny" Volume One ~ The Mind of Christ"**, available on Amazon as Kindle Format, IBook's, and hard copy very reasonable priced. Copies also available at the church.
- **Under the New Birth GAPIW Kingdom Fellowship,** they also trains and ordains men and women commissioning them to ministry. They are the founders of New Birth Global Apostolic Prophetic in Warfare Kingdom Fellowship that oversees those being trained and ordained under their covering.

  - **Currently, they are the overseers,** "Women of Worth" Ministry, Prayer and Evangelism ministry in Jamaica founder: - Minister (Pastor-Elect) Georgia Nicholas-Green and five (5) churches in the Philippines.

  - **The fellowship is also a ministerial alliance for fivefold ministers/leaders desiring covering for their ministry/church**

- **April 2013** ~ The Prophetic in Warfare Deliverance and Worship Tabernacle School of the Prophets and Biblical Studies was launched offering training for five-fold leaders, as well as intercessors, armor bearers/adjutant equip them to standing as "God's General" in Intercession.

- In **May 2013** ~ Apostle Nadine and Pastor Richard Manning (deceased) ~ established the ***"Blog Talk Radio Show"*** offering words of Prophetic Insight and Revelatory Knowledge empowering the body of Christ through Prolific, prophetic teaching and preaching flow with Prophetic Declarations.
- The show has now migrated to a national radio show as **"LET THE PROPHET SPEAK"** hosted on Liftfm Radio based in Bridgeton.

  - o Listen in the Bridgeton, NJ area at: 98.5 FM

  - o Listen in the Wildwood and Cape May, NJ areas at: 97.9 FM

  - o Listen in Millville and Vineland, NJ areas at: 103.3 FM

  - o Listen online anytime at: www.liftfm.com

  - o **You can also find Apostle Nadine Manning and Pastor Richard Manning on www.spreaker.com, www.youtube.com , @ www.twitter.com – @Apostlenadine or @PropheticinWDWT or and on their ministry page www.globalpropheticinwarfaremininstries.com for more of their Ministry Messages**
  - o Apostle Nadine Manning also has a writer's blog on Wordpress.com as: - http://apostlenadinemanning.wordpress.com or www.apostlenadineglobal.com.

or www.globalpropheticinwarfareministries.com

- **June 22, 2013** ~ 1st Graduation and Ordination Service of the Prophetic in Warfare Deliverance and Worship Tabernacle School of the Prophets and Biblical Studies
- **In three (3) years** ~ The ministry annually hosted three (3 Prophetic Watch of the Lord Summits and Prophetic Ingathering of God's Army Summits, a prophetic gathering assembling the body of Christ from various regions.
- **September 2013** ~ the Prophetic Watch of the Lord Summit migrated into a Paradigm shift called **"The Prophetic Watchman Alert Summit",** we had people travelling from Jamaica just to be at this conferences. One person was issued an emergency visa just to be there.
- **September 2013** ~ Apostle, Dr. Nadine Manning also published several booklets such as the Watchman Alert Prologue, and Prophetic in Warfare Handbook, CD's and DVD's on the Preaching and teaching ministry is also available.
- **November 2013** ~ Apostle, Dr. Nadine and Pastor, Dr. Richard established the Prophetic Company of Tribes Newsletter to bridge the gap between the church and the local community businesses and organizations. This was launched in our Annual Ingathering of God's Army Conference in November 2013.
- **In November 2013** ~ Prophetic in Warfare Deliverance and Worship Tabernacle has reached

a landmark in feeding 101 families through our Men with A Mission Food Pantry.

- **Since April 2010 to present** ~ Not known to many, Apostle Dr. Nadine is a dynamic cook, and one of her youth, Elijah Milbourne calls her ***"The God Chef"*** she offers catering, as well as Dinner and Lunch Platters through their "Jamerican Taste Cuisine Business.

- Apostle, Dr. Nadine Manning, the Late, Pastor, Dr. Richard Manning (deceased) and the children wrote many songs of deliverances that they sang in our ministry and at various events we host at our church.

Their children has a group called ***"The Joshua Tribes"*** launched in June 2013!

- Apostle, Dr. Nadine Manning is a singing preacher, singing songs of deliverances and has also ministered several times with her own songs at other churches over the last 20 years and has over 15 songs of her own soon to be released.

- **January 2014** ~ Apostle, Dr. Nadine Manning is a Life Empowerment Coaches – Offering counselling sessions and spiritual/Christian Word Based Therapy to those who need one and one ministering, empowerment and deliverance.

- **February 2014:- Phase 2 of "The Ingathering of God's Army"** was held on church grounds: - Hosting Guest Speaker and Missionaries from Toronto, Canada.

- **August 2014:-** The Launch of "Mega-Mind ~ Mega-Kingdom was held as a two (2) day conference in Spanish Town, Jamaica

Thanks Be To the Lord

- God has truly granted this ministry favor with men and with God according to Luke 2:52, despite the challenges, they have certainly overcome and achieved these great triumphs in ministry.
- God has truly manifested His presence with Glory Cloud and visible witness of His miracles, signs and wonders captured on camera in this ministry!
- **To God be all the Glory and all The Honor; It Belongs To Him!!!**

A Publication of

Apostle Dr. Nadine Manning Global Ministries Inc.

(1)   Awake To Your Destiny – Volume 1
~ "The Mind of Christ."

(2)   "I Am Anointed For This." – Awake To Your Destiny – Volume 2.

****Sermons and Prophetic Prayer Teaching and Declaration available on CDs and DVDs****

You can write, call our email me at:-
Apostle Dr. Nadine Manning

P.O. Box 343, Millville, New Jersey 08332.

Email: - *apostlenadineglobal@gmail.com or nadinehmanning@gmail.com.*

Website: - ***Apostlenadineglobal.com or www.globalpropheticinwarfareministries.com***

Telephone: - 609-972-6346 or 856-825-8280.

Contact Us

Apostle, Dr. Nadine Manning Bookings for: - Preaching/Teaching, Conferences, Workshops, Revivals or Spiritual Warfare and Deliverance Prayer Services or Revivals, please email us at *Apostlenadineglobal@gmail.com* or *propheticinwarfare@gmail.com.* Or you may call us at

Telephone #s: - 609-972-6346 or 856-825-8280.